MOVIELISTS

JOHN KOSKI is Associate Editor of *YOU* Magazine. He has been a journalist for twenty years, three of which were spent as a film critic.

MITCHELL SYMONS is an author and journalist who writes for a variety of publications, including a regular column in *Punch*. An avid movie buff, he used to direct *Film '81*, has written extensively about films and once wrote a screenplay that was so awful it never saw the light of day.

£3 —

Anc

22/4

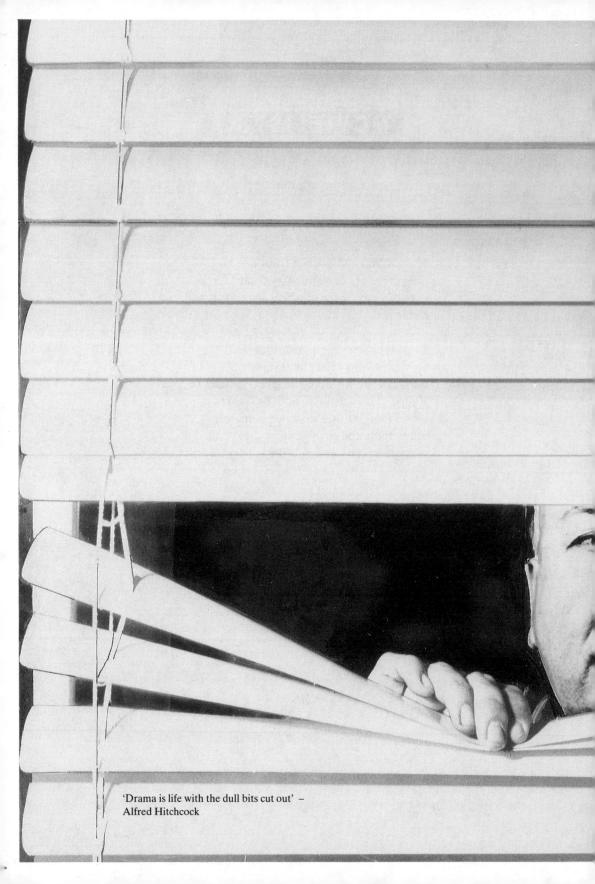

'Drama is life with the dull bits cut out' –
Alfred Hitchcock

MOVIELISTS

John Koski and Mitchell Symons

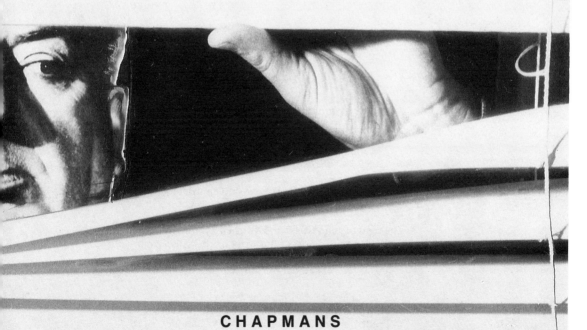

CHAPMANS

Chapmans Publishers Ltd
141–143 Drury Lane
London WC2B 5TB

First published by Chapmans 1992

ISBN 1–85592–726–8

A CIP catalogue record of this book is available
from the British Library

Photoset in Linotron Times by
MC Typeset Ltd, Wouldham, Rochester, Kent
Printed in England by Clays Ltd, St Ives plc

ACKNOWLEDGEMENTS

The authors would like to thank Sara Driver and
Patricia Martin for their invaluable research and
Donnie and Alison Kerr for their invaluable lists.

PICTURE CREDITS

The photographs in this book are reproduced by
courtesy of Associated Newspapers Ltd and the
following: 9, Lucasfilm; 11, People in Pictures;
15, Taliafilm; 20, Touchstone Pictures; 21,
Warner Bros; 27, Warner Bros; 30, London
Features International; 31, Fox Photos; 33,
United Artists Corporation; 35, Tri-Star
Pictures; 37, Orion; 39, Knockout Ltd; 40,
Tom Wargacki; 41, Orion; 42, Guild Film;
45, Paramount Pictures Corporation; 48, United
Artists Corporation; 49, London Features
International; 52, Universal City Studios;
53, Universal International; 55, UPP, Twentieth
Century Fox Film Corporation; 56, United
Artists Corporation; 58, World-Icon, NV;
61, National Film Archive; 64, Tri-Star Pictures;
65, Pathé Entertainment; 66, Warner Bros,
Columbia Picture Industries, Twentieth Century
Fox Film Corporation; 67, Rex Features;
70, Twentieth Century Fox Film Corporation;
71, Fox Films; 78, The Walt Disney Company;
84, London Features International; 86, Universal
City Studios; 89, Paramount Pictures Corporation;
90, United Artists Corporation; 91, Twentieth
Century Fox Film Corporation; 92, Cinema
International Corporation; 93, Warner Bros.

The publishers acknowledge the rights of the
copyright holders in the illustrations throughout
this work.

CONTENTS

You've got to start somewhere – ten roles stars would probably prefer to forget

Clint Eastwood's first role was as a lab technician in *Revenge of the Creature* (1955)

Harrison Ford made his début as a bellboy in *Dead Heat on a Merry-Go-Round* (1966)

Jane Fonda made her film début as a cheerleader in *Tall Story* (1960)

Robert Vaughn played the title role in *Teenage Caveman* (1958)

Jack Nicholson played a masochistic dental patient in *The Little Shop of Horrors* (1961)

Sean Connery was a diamond scavenger in *Tarzan's Greatest Adventure* (1959)

Donald Sutherland made his début in a dual role: as a soldier and (in drag) as a witch in *Castle of the Living Dead* (1964)

Debra Winger played Lynda Carter's younger sister in the TV series *Wonder Woman* (1976)

Charles Bronson played a grotesque deaf-mute in *House of Wax* (1953)

Mel Gibson's first role was as a surfer in *Summer City* (1976)

Harrison, the bellboy who made good

Anne and Dustin, coming of age in *The Graduate*

Ten things we know about America from watching the movies

Nobody ever eats more than one mouthful from a plate of food

Every platoon has at least one person who can play the mouth-organ

All young boys can reach their bedroom by climbing a convenient tree

Restaurants offer at least six different kinds of toast for breakfast

Nobody ever locks their car

The bedroom curtains are always left open at night

If there's a storm, the bedroom window is left open as well

Everybody goes to school until the age of thirty

When people fall in love they go shopping in the local street market

Paper boys never need to get off their bicycles

Act your age – ten improbable parents

Sean Connery, 58, played the father of Harrison Ford, 46, in *Indiana Jones and the Last Crusade* (1989)

Angela Lansbury was 37 when she played the mother of 34-year-old Laurence Harvey in *The Manchurian Candidate* (1962)

In *Weeds*, Anne Ramsey, 58, plays the mother of Nick Nolte, 46 (1985)

And in *Throw Momma from the Train*, Anne Ramsey, 58, plays the mother of Danny De Vito, 43 (1987)

When Cary Grant made *North by Northwest*, he was 55. His mother, played by Jessie Royce Landis, was 54 (1959)

Blair Brown and Mark Harmon were 39 and 36 when they played mother and son in *Stealing Home* (1988)

In *Beaches*, Lainie Kazan, 45, plays the mother of Bette Midler, 42 (1988)

In *The Graduate*, Katharine Ross, who was 25, played the daughter of Anne Bancroft, 36 (1967)

And in *The Colbys*, Katharine Ross, then 43, was the mother of John James, 29 (1985)

Sean Connery, 58, played the father of Dustin Hoffman, 51, in *Family Business* (1989)

It's a wrap – ten memorable last lines of movies

'Louis, I think this is the beginning of a beautiful friendship' (Humphrey Bogart in *Casablanca*, 1942)

'Look, Ma, top of the world' (James Cagney in *White Heat*, 1949)

'Marry me, Emily, and I'll never look at any other horse' (Groucho Marx in *A Day at the Races*, 1937)

'Oh, Jerry, don't let's ask for the moon. We have the stars' (Bette Davis in *Now Voyager*, 1942)

'Tomorrow is another day' (Vivien Leigh in *Gone with the Wind*, 1939)

'Good, for a minute I thought we were in trouble' (Paul Newman in *Butch Cassidy and the Sundance Kid*, 1969)

'Oh, Aunt Em, there's no place like home' (Judy Garland in *The Wizard of Oz*, 1939)

'All right, Mr De Mille, I'm ready for my close-up' (Gloria Swanson in *Sunset Boulevard*, 1950)

'I now pronounce you men and wives' (Ian Wolfe in *Seven Brides for Seven Brothers*, 1954)

'The lobsters are back!' (Michael Craig in *High Tide at Noon*, 1957)

Do not adjust your set – ten black-and-white movies made in the last 20 years

Broadway Danny Rose (1984)
Dead Men Don't Wear Plaid (1982)
The Elephant Man (1980)
Stardust Memories (1980)
Raging Bull (1980)
Manhattan (1979)
Eraserhead (1978)
Hester Street (1975)
Young Frankenstein (1974)
Paper Moon (1973)

Butch and Sundance, all wrapped up

It's never too late – ten delayed movie sequels

The Wizard of Oz (1939), *Return to Oz* (1985): 46 years

The Maltese Falcon (1941), *The Black Bird* (1975): 34 years

National Velvet (1945), *International Velvet* (1978): 33 years

High Noon (1952), *High Noon Part II: The Return of Will Kane* (1980): 28 years

The Hustler (1961), *The Color of Money* (1986): 25 years

Psycho (1960), *Psycho II* (1983): 23 years

The Ghost in the Invisible Bikini (1966), *Back to the Beach* (1987): 21 years

The Last Picture Show (1971), *Texasville* (1990): 19 years

2001: A Space Odyssey (1968), *2010* (1984): 16 years

The Godfather II (1974), *The Godfather III* (1990): 16 years

Ten movies that combine black-and-white and colour

The Wizard of Oz (1939): the land of Oz is in colour

The Women (1939): fashion show in colour

The Moon and Sixpence (1942): the fire at the end is in colour

The Picture of Dorian Gray (1945): the picture at the end is in colour

A Matter of Life and Death (1946): earth is in colour

The Solid Gold Cadillac (1956): the final shots of the title car are in colour

Zelig (1983): the modern-day interviews are in colour

She's Gotta Have It (1986): colour sequence in a park

In Bed With Madonna (1991): the stage show is in colour

If . . . (1969): mixes black and white with colour throughout

Love according to the script

'Love means never having to say you're sorry' (Ryan O'Neal in *Love Story*, 1970)

'Love is like the measles – you only get it once and the older you are, the tougher it goes' (Howard Keel in *Seven Brides for Seven Brothers*, 1954)

'Love is a romantic designation for a most ordinary biological – or, shall we say, chemical – process' (Greta Garbo in *Ninotchka*, 1939)

'I love him because he's the kind of guy who gets drunk on buttermilk' (Barbara Stanwyck in *Ball of Fire*, 1942)

'Love is a miracle. It's like a birthmark – you can't hide it' (George Segal in *Blume in Love*, 1973)

'Maybe love is like luck – you have to go all the way to find it' (Robert Mitchum in *Out of the Past*, 1947)

'Send roses to room 424 and put "Emily, I love you" on the back of the bill' (Groucho Marx in *A Night in Casablanca*, 1946)

'Love is for the very young' (Kirk Douglas in *The Bad and the Beautiful*, 1952)

'You don't know what love means. To you, it's just another four-letter word' (Paul Newman in *Cat on a Hot Tin Roof*, 1958)

'Love isn't something you can put on or take off like an overcoat' (Arthur Kennedy in *Champion*, 1949)

Ten film endings which were changed before being released

Fatal Attraction (1987): Glenn Close committed suicide and Michael Douglas was charged with her murder

Pretty Woman (1990): Julia Roberts walked out on Richard Gere

A Fish Called Wanda (1988): Jamie Lee Curtis took the jewels, abandoned John Cleese and flew to South America alone

The War of the Roses (1989): Michael Douglas and Kathleen Turner murdered each other

A Kiss Before Dying (1991): Matt Dillon died in a cauldron of molten copper

Turner and Hooch (1989): Hooch lived on instead of being shot

Blade Runner (1982): It was suggested that Harrison Ford was a replicant rather than a human

Double Indemnity (1944): Two final scenes, showing Fred MacMurray being tried and sent to the gas chamber, were cut

Rocky (1976): Sylvester Stallone walked out of the empty boxing arena hand-in-hand with Talia Shire, rather than pushing through the crowds to embrace her

Dying Young (1991): Julia Roberts drove away with the handsome boy next door

Julia, the pretty woman who nearly walked out on Richard Gere

Politicians who appeared in movies

Benito Mussolini as an extra in *The Eternal City* (1914)

Michael Foot as himself in *Rockets Galore* (1958)

Fidel Castro as an extra in *Holiday in Mexico* (1946)

Ed Koch as himself in *The Muppets Take Manhattan* (1984)

Jomo Kenyatta as an African chief in *Sanders of the River* (1935)

Leon Trotsky in a bit part in *My Official Wife* (1914)

Gough Whitlam as himself in *Barry McKenzie Holds His Own* (1974)

Yitzhak Rabin as himself in *Operation Thunderbolt* (1977)

Hubert Humphrey as himself in *The Candidate* (1972)

Theodore Roosevelt as himself in *Womanhood, The Glory of a Nation* (1917)

Movies within movies I – ten movies that contain cinema screenings of real films

Bonnie and Clyde (1967) features *Gold Diggers of 1933* (1933)

Two Weeks in Another Town (1962) features *The Bad and the Beautiful* (1952)

The Last Picture Show (1971) features *Red River* (1948) and *Father of the Bride* (1950)

Hannah and Her Sisters (1986) features *Duck Soup* (1933)

Throw Momma From the Train (1987) features *Strangers on a Train* (1951)

Summer of '42 (1971) features *Now Voyager* (1942)

Cinema Paradiso (1988) features *Modern Times* (1936)

Play It Again Sam (1972) features *Casablanca* (1942)

Annie Hall (1977) features *The Sorrow and the Pity* (1970)

Crimes and Misdemeanours (1990) features *Mr and Mrs Smith* (1941)

Movies within movies II – ten movies that contain TV screenings of real films

Pretty Woman (1990) features *Charade* (1963)

The Fabulous Baker Boys (1989) features *It's a Wonderful Life* (1946)

Look Who's Talking (1989) features *It's a Wonderful Life* (1946)

Gremlins (1984) features *It's a Wonderful Life* (1946)

Home Alone (1990) features *It's a Wonderful Life* (1946), dubbed into French

When Harry Met Sally . . . (1989) features *Casablanca* (1942)

Field of Dreams (1989) features *Harvey* (1950)

Walk, Don't Run (1966) features *Two Rode Together* (1961), dubbed into Japanese

Conquest of Space (1955) features *Here Come the Girls* (1953)

Whatever Happened to Baby Jane? (1962) features *Sadie McKee* (1934)

Ten movie howlers

An electric street lamp is seen in *Gone with the Wind* (1939)

In *Anatomy of a Murder* Lee Remick is seen sitting in a café wearing a dress. When she leaves it she's wearing trousers (1959)

An Inter-City train is visible in *Quadrophenia* – set before they were around (1979)

In Steven Spielberg's TV film *Duel*, the camera can be seen reflected in the glass of a phonebox (1972)

In *Jagged Edge* Glenn Close is seen arriving in court wearing a grey suit. A few minutes later the suit is blue. By the end of the scene the suit has also been brown (1985)

In *Raiders of the Lost Ark* a map can be seen with Thailand marked on it. When the film was set Thailand was still called Siam (1981)

In *Falling in Love* starring Meryl Streep and Robert de Niro, a camera can be clearly seen reflected (1984)

TV aerials can be seen on the roofs of houses in *The Wrong Box*, which is set in the nineteenth century (1966)

Two VW Beetles can be spotted in *The Prisoner of Zenda*, which was also set in the nineteenth century (1979)

In *Rich and Famous*, Jacqueline Bisset boards a Boeing 747 – years before the plane was in use (1981)

Ten creative places to do it in the movies

In the surf (*From Here To Eternity*) 1953

On the kitchen table (*The Postman Always Rings Twice*) 1981

In an aeroplane lavatory (*Emmanuelle*) 1974

In an elevator (*Fatal Attraction*) 1987

In the back of a chauffeur-driven limo (*No Way Out*) 1986

On the hall carpet (*Body Heat*) 1981

In an alleyway (*9½ Weeks*) 1986

On a grand piano (*Pretty Woman*) 1990

In the rain (*Lady Chatterley's Lover*) 1981

Floating in a spaceship (*Barbarella*) 1967

Goldfinger – Bond villain who got taken for a sucker

No, not tonight, James – Ursula

Ten things Bond villains always say

'How nice to meet you, Meester Bond'
'You have no chance of escape, you understand'
'It's so nice to have some civilised company for a change'
'You amuse me, Meester Bond'
'Do you approve of the wine?'
'You have been an irritant for too long'
'Unfortunately your predecessor cannot be with us tonight'
'I hope you don't mind being my guest tonight'
'Shaken, not stirred. Am I correct?'
''Bye, 'bye, Meester Bond'

Ten things Bond girls always say

'I never knew it could be like this'
'Who's that man in our bathroom?'
'Oh, Jems, hold me'
'I have the master tape here in my bikini'
'Do be careful, darling. I don't want you to get into any trouble'
'Have there been many other women?'
'He forced me to work for him, and I was so frightened'
'I have had to fend for myself since I was a child'
'You're the first real man I've ever met'
'You fix the drinks and I'll slip into something more comfortable'

Ten films directed by Alan Smithee, a pseudonym used by directors who don't like what the studio has done to their masterworks

The television release of *Dune* (1988): David Lynch
Death of a Gunfighter (1969): Don Siegel
Student Bodies (1981): Michael Ritchie
Let's Get Harry (1986): Stuart Rosenberg
Riviera (1987): John Frankenheimer
City in Fear (1980): Jud Taylor
Moonlight (1982): Jackie Cooper
Morgan Stewart's Coming Home (1987): Paul Aaron
Stitches (1985): Rod Holcomb
Catchfire (1989): Dennis Hopper

Take one! Ten actors who had an isolated attempt at directing

Anthony Quinn: *The Buccaneer* (1958)
Charles Laughton: *Night of the Hunter* (1955)
Albert Finney: *Charlie Bubbles* (1967)
Larry Hagman: *Beware! The Blob* (1972)
Richard Harris: *Bloomfield* (1969)
Charlton Heston: *Antony and Cleopatra* (1972)
Anthony Perkins: *Psycho III* (1986)
Diane Keaton: *Heaven* (1986)
Patrick McGoohan: *Catch My Soul* (1973)
Jack Lemmon: *Kotch* (1971)

Take two! Ten directors who remade their own movies

Frank Capra: *Lady for a Day* (1933); *Pocketful of Miracles* (1961)
Alfred Hitchcock: *The Man Who Knew Too Much* (1934 and 1956)
Raoul Walsh: *Strawberry Blonde* (1941); *One Sunday Afternoon* (1948)
Howard Hawks: *Ball of Fire* (1941); *A Song is Born* (1948)
Leo McCarey: *Love Affair* (1939); *An Affair to Remember* (1957)
Cecil B. DeMille: *The Ten Commandments* (1923 and 1956)
John Ford: *Judge Priest* (1934); *The Sun Shines Bright* (1953)
Ernst Lubitsch: *The Marriage Circle* (1924); *One Hour With You* (1932)
Frank Capra: *Broadway Bill* (1934); *Riding High* (1950)
D.W. Griffith: *The Battle of the Sexes* (1914 and 1928)

Seeing double – ten stars who have played both twins in a movie

Jeremy Irons (Elliot and Beverley Mantle in *Dead Ringers*, 1988)
Hayley Mills (Sharon McKendrick and Susan Evers in *The Parent Trap*, 1961)
Sean Young (Ellen and Dorothy Carlsson in *A Kiss Before Dying*, 1990)
Bette Midler (Sadie Shelton and Sadie Ratliff in *Big Business*, 1988)
Olivia de Havilland (Ruth and Terry Collins in *The Dark Mirror*, 1946)
Bette Davis (Kate and Patricia Bosworth in *A Stolen Life*, 1946)
Meg Ryan (Angelica and Patricia Graynamore in *Joe Versus the Volcano*, 1990)
Gene Wilder (Claude and Philippe in *Start the Revolution Without Me*, 1969)
Boris Karloff (Anton and Grigor Berghmann in *The Black Room*, 1935)
Betty Hutton (Susie and Rosemary Allison in *Here Come the Waves*, 1944)

Ten things American cops do in the movies

Go for 72 hours without sleep
Argue with their ex-wives
Have a partner who is happily married
Eat hotdogs while driving
Address any woman they meet as 'lady'
Wear a gun while asleep
Fall in love with female suspects
Drink plenty of alcohol
Take leave so they can complete the case – *their* way – in their own time
Treat the police commissioner like dirt

Olympic medallists who became actors (however briefly)

Johnny Weissmuller, star of countless Tarzan films, won seven swimming golds at the 1924 and 1928 Games

Buster Crabbe, 1932 swimming gold medallist, became better known playing Flash Gordon

Sonja Henie, skating gold medallist in 1928, 1932, and 1936, went on to appear in a series of Hollywood musicals

Herman Brix, 1928 silver medallist in the shotput, starred in two Tarzan films

Rafer Johnson, 1960 decathlon gold medallist, gave a number of unmemorable performances

Sharron Davies, silver medallist in the 1980, 400m individual swimming medley, starred in a silent comedy called *The Optimist*

Glenn Morris, 1936 gold medallist in the decathlon, starred in action movies

Muhammad Ali, who as Cassius Clay won a boxing gold at the 1960 Games, starred in the autobiographical picture, *The Greatest*

Bob Mathias, winner of the decathlon title in 1948 and 1952, enjoyed a brief movie career before becoming a US Congressman

Bruce Jenner, winner of the decathlon in 1976, flopped in films and appeared in the TV series CHiPs

Ten lines you'd hear only in a Hollywood biopic

'You'll never finish that symphony the way you're going, Schubert'

'Can Benjamin come out kite flying, Mrs Franklin?'

'How many times do I have to tell you, Ludwig? Are you going deaf or something?'

'You must be mad if you think anyone's going to buy those, Vincent'

'Leave Stratford, Will, and make all the world your stage'

'Remember, Abe, you can't fool all of the people all of the time'

'How much longer are you going to be in that bathroom, Archimedes?'

'Come, Comrade Marx, let's go gambling – we have nothing to lose but our change'

'Tonight, Napoleon?'

'George, what do you know about this cherry tree?'

Ten novelists who've appeared in movies

Saul Bellow: *Zelig* (1983)

Damon Runyon: *The Great White Way* (1924)

Sir Arthur Conan Doyle: *The $5,000,000 Counterfeiting Plot* (1914)

Jean-Paul Sartre: *La vie commence demain* (1952)

Mickey Spillane: *Ring of Fear* (1954)

Mark Twain: *A Curious Dream* (1907)

William Burroughs: *It Don't Pay to be an Honest Citizen* (1985)

G.K. Chesterton: *Rosy Rapture – The Pride of the Beauty Chorus* (1914)

Graham Greene: *Day for Night* (1973)

Norman Mailer: *Wild 90* (1968); *Beyond the Law* (1968); *Maidstone* (1970); *Ragtime* (1981); *King Lear* (1987)

Write your own movie script – ten classic lines you'll need

'You've got it all figured out, haven't you?'

'You're no good. You never were and you never will be'

'You big lug – don't you see it's because I love you?'

'Listen and listen good!'

'You are either a very brave man – or a very stupid one'

'Why are you telling me all this?'

'I don't like it – it's too quiet'

'This one's for Johnny'

'Let's get outta this place!'

'You'd better wise up – and wise up fast'

Actors who've cross-dressed in movies

Greta Garbo (*Queen Christina*, 1933)

Dustin Hoffman (*Tootsie*, 1982)

Jack Lemmon (*Some Like It Hot*, 1959)

Anthony Perkins (*Psycho*, 1960)

Barbra Streisand (*Yentl*, 1983)

Katharine Hepburn (*Sylvia Scarlett*, 1935)

Alec Guinness (*Kind Hearts and Coronets*, 1949)

Julie Andrews (*Victor, Victoria*, 1982)

Alastair Sim (*The Belles of St Trinian's*, 1954)

Margaret Lockwood (*The Wicked Lady*, 1945)

Alec Guinness, cross and dressed – in *Kind Hearts and Coronets*

Gene Kelly, happy to sing about Hollywood even in the rain

Ten Hollywood movies about Hollywood

A Star is Born (1937, 1954)
Sunset Boulevard (1950)
The Bad and the Beautiful (1952)
Singing in the Rain (1952)
Silent Movie (1976)
Postcards from the Edge (1990)
The Lost Squadron (1932)
The Oscar (1966)
The Day of the Locust (1974)
The Last Tycoon (1976)

Ten movies based on Shakespeare

West Side Story (1961): *Romeo and Juliet*
Prospero's Books (1991): *The Tempest*
Joe Macbeth (1955): *Macbeth*
The Boys From Syracuse (1940): *The Comedy of Errors*
A Double Life (1947): *Othello*
Carry On Cleo (1964): *Antony and Cleopatra*
The Dresser (1983): *King Lear*
Kiss Me Kate (1953): *The Taming of the Shrew*
An Honourable Murder (1959): *Julius Caesar*
Forbidden Planet (1956): *The Tempest*

Loony tunes: Roger, Bob, Jessica – and Amy

Dub, dub, dub – stars whose singing was done by someone else

Audrey Hepburn in *My Fair Lady* (Marni Nixon, 1964)

Leslie Caron in *Gigi* (Betty Wand, 1958)

Cyd Charisse in *Brigadoon* (Carole Richards, 1954)

Christopher Plummer in *The Sound of Music* (Bill Lee, 1965)

Lauren Bacall in *To Have and Have Not* (Andy Williams, 1945)

Rita Hayworth in *Pal Joey* (Jo Ann Greer, 1957)

Rosanno Brazzi in *South Pacific* (Giorgio Tozzi, 1958)

Ava Gardner in *Showboat* (Annette Warren, 1951)

Rosalind Russell in *Gypsy* (Lisa Kirk, 1962)

Jessica Rabbit in *Who Framed Roger Rabbit* (Amy Irving, 1988)

Ten journalists who've appeared in movies

Clive James: *Barry McKenzie Holds His Own* (1977)

Michael Parkinson: *Madhouse* (1974)

Malcolm Muggeridge: *Heavens Above* (1963)

Arthur Christiansen: *The Day the Earth Caught Fire* (1961)

Bernard Levin: *Nothing but the Best* (1963)

Godfrey Winn: *Billy Liar* (1963)

David Robinson: *If . . .* (1960)

David Frost: *The VIPs* (1963)

Richard Dimbleby: *Libel* (1959)

Joan Bakewell: *The Touchables* (1967)

Those who are about to die – ten movie lines that tell you someone's about to be bumped off

'Let's split up and I'll search the cellar'

'Of course I'll marry you, 007'

'Why did you bring me all the way up here?'

'I'm getting out of this place first thing in the morning'

'Hello, operator, I've been cut off. Hello, operator?'

'Oh, it's only you. Come in'

'Why are you looking at me like that?'

'Don't worry, you're safe now'

'So it was you all along'

'There's no way anyone can get in now'

Not Guilty, Your Honour – De Niro in Scorsese's *Goodfellas*

You had to be there – ten movie 'in' jokes

The Godfather II (1974): Troy Donahue's character is named Merle Johnson – the actor's own real name

The Black Cat (1941): someone says of Basil Rathbone's character: 'He thinks he's Sherlock Holmes!' – he had just begun a long-running series playing the sleuth

His Girl Friday (1940): Cary Grant mentions a man named Archie Leach, his own real name

The Spoilers (1942): a drunk being thrown out of a hotel is given the name of the film's associate producer, Lee Marcus

Bedazzled (1967): Dudley Moore's character is called Stanley Moon, the name by which John Gielgud mistakenly introduced him to friends

Sleuth (1972): director Joseph Mankiewicz gives screen billing to 'Eve Channing', an amalgam of two characters from his big success *All About Eve* (1950) – but only Laurence Olivier and Michael Caine appear in the film

The Commitments (1991): One name suggested for the group is The Likely Lads, the hit TV series written by the film's scriptwriters, Dick Clement and Ian la Frenais

The Road to Hong Kong (1962): Bob Hope's character is called Chester Babcock, the real name of songwriter Jimmy Van Heusen

One, Two, Three (1961): James Cagney threatens to push a grapefruit in someone's face – a reference to his 1931 classic *The Public Enemy* – and a clock chimes 'Yankee Doodle Dandy' – another of his earlier hits

In most of his films, David Niven manages to mention someone named Trubshawe – a running gag with his actor pal Michael Trubshawe

A guide to directors

Bergmanesque: grey and depressing

Wenders-like: colourful and depressing

Capraesque: sentimental but sharp

Scorseseian: Catholic guilt

Allenesque: Jewish guilt

Hitchcockian: the director makes a cameo appearance

Lynch-like: could be significant, but who can tell?

Bertoluccian: floral

Spielbergish: childish plot, adult budget

Cormanesque: adult plot, childish budget

All in the family – parents who appeared in movies with their children

Ryan O'Neal and Tatum: *Paper Moon* (1973)
Henry Fonda and Jane: *On Golden Pond* (1981)
Martin Sheen and Charlie: *Wall Street* (1987)
Vanessa Redgrave and Joely Richardson:
  Wetherby (1985)
Ingrid Bergman and Isabella Rossellini: *A Matter of Time* (1976)
Walter Huston and John: *The Treasure of the Sierra Madre* (1948)
John Mills and Hayley: *Tiger Bay* (1959)
Maureen O'Sullivan and Mia Farrow: *Hannah and Her Sisters* (1985)
Judy Garland and Liza Minnelli: *In the Good Old Summertime* (1949)
Jack Palance and Cody: *Young Guns* (1988)

Ten real-life relationships translated to the screen

Margaux and Mariel Hemingway: sisters in *Lipstick* (1976)
Dennis and Randy Quaid: brothers in *The Long Riders* (1980)
James and Jeanne Cagney: brother and sister in *Yankee Doodle Dandy* (1942)
Diane Cilento and Jason Connery: mother and son in *The Boy Who Had Everything* (1984)
Priscilla Pointer and Amy Irving: mother and daughter in *Carrie* (1976)
Raymond and Daniel Massey: father and son in *The Queen's Guards* (1960)
Michael and Vanessa Redgrave: father and daughter in *Behind the Mask* (1958)
Madhur and Sakeena Jaffrey: mother and daughter in *The Perfect Murder* (1988)
Geoffrey and Felicity Kendal: father and daughter in *Shakespeare Wallah* (1965)
Diane Ladd and Laura Dern: mother and daughter in *Wild at Heart* (1990)

'Action, dearest!' Ten men who have directed their wives in movies

Mel Brooks (Anne Bancroft in *Silent Movie*, 1976)
Tony Richardson (Vanessa Redgrave in *The Charge of the Light Brigade*, 1968)
Orson Welles (Rita Hayworth in *The Lady from Shanghai*, 1948)
Bryan Forbes (Nanette Newman in *Séance on a Wet Afternoon*, 1964)
John Cassavetes (Gena Rowlands in *A Woman under the Influence*, 1974)
Roman Polanski (Sharon Tate in *The Fearless Vampire Killers*, 1967)
Charlie Chaplin (Paulette Goddard in *Modern Times*, 1936)
Paul Newman (Joanne Woodward in *Rachel, Rachel*, 1968)
Vincente Minnelli (Judy Garland in *The Pirate*, 1948)
Anthony Newley (Joan Collins in *Can Hieronymus Merkin Ever Forget Mercy Humppe and Find True Happiness?*, 1969)

Making her camera debut – baby Liza with mother Judy

Penn and Madonna, striped for action

Married times – Chaplin and Goddard

Ten movies starring married couples

Shanghai Surprise (Sean Penn and Madonna, 1986)

I Want a Divorce (Dick Powell and Joan Blondell, 1940)

The Reformer and the Redhead (Dick Powell and June Allyson, 1950)

Who's Afraid of Virginia Woolf? (Elizabeth Taylor and Richard Burton, 1966)

Go into Your Dance (Ruby Keeler and Al Jolson, 1935)

The Big Sleep (Lauren Bacall and Humphrey Bogart, 1946)

Witness for the Prosecution (Elsa Lanchester and Charles Laughton, 1957)

Modern Times (Charlie Chaplin and Paulette Goddard, 1936)

That Hamilton Woman (Vivien Leigh and Laurence Olivier, 1941)

The Lady from Shanghai (Orson Welles and Rita Hayworth, 1948)

Shock, horror! Ten women who've taken their clothes off in movies

Helen Mirren: *Savage Messiah* (1972)
Ellen Barkin: *Siesta* (1987)
Glenda Jackson: *Women in Love* (1969)
Valerie Perrine: *Lenny* (1974)
Julie Andrews: *S.O.B.* (1981)
Patsy Kensit: *Lethal Weapon 2* (1989)
Amanda Donohoe: *Castaway* (1986)
Bo Derek: *10* (1979)
Maria Schneider: *Last Tango in Paris* (1972)
Joan Collins: *The Bitch* (1979)

Ten men who've taken their clothes off in movies

Ryan O'Neal: *Partners* (1982)
Al Pacino: *Scarecrow* (1973)
Treat Williams: *Hair* (1979)
Dustin Hoffman: *Marathon Man* (1976)
Jeff Bridges: *Winter Kills* (1979)
Oliver Reed: *Castaway* (1986)
Don Johnson: *The Magic Garden of Stanley Sweetheart* (1970)
Alan Bates: *Women in Love* (1969)
Malcolm McDowell: *Caligula* (1979)
William Hurt: *Body Heat* (1981)

All our yesterdays – ten things we know about 1950s England from Ealing comedies

The strongest swear word was 'damn'
Men weren't allowed to join the police force until the age of 30
Cockneys said 'Cor, love a duck' in every sentence
There was no sex before marriage
It never rained
No criminal ever got away with his crime
Racy 'young' men were all over 40
The more beautiful a girl was, the more upper-class her accent
All men over 60 smoked pipes
All men knew how to drive trains

Schlock, horror! Two out of ten for Bo and Dud

Take one – ten childish movie débuts of movie stars

Beau Bridges: *No Minor Vices* (1948) aged seven
Jeff Bridges: *The Company She Keeps* (1949) aged two
Natalie Wood: *Happy Land* (1943) aged five
Rita Moreno: *Silk Legs* (1936) aged five
Ron Howard: *The Journey* (1958) aged five
Liza Minnelli: *In the Good Old Summertime* (1949) aged three
Bruce Lee: *The Birth of Mankind* (1946) aged six
Jodie Foster: *Napoleon and Samantha* (1971) aged eight
Juliet Mills: *In Which We Serve* (1941) aged one
Cyril Cusack: *Knocknagow* (1918) aged eight

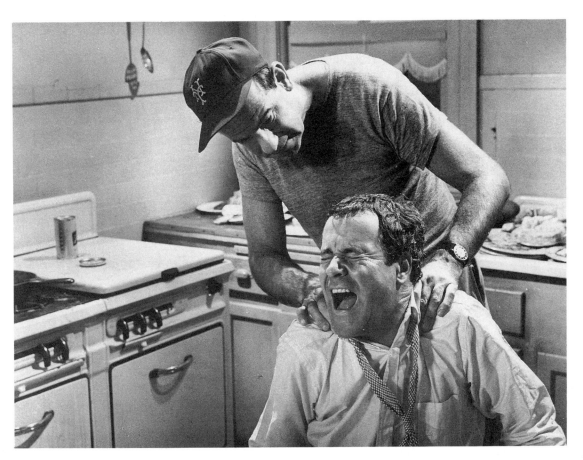

Ten movies that became TV sitcoms

The Odd Couple (1968)
House Calls (1978)
M.A.S.H. (1970)
Nine to Five (1980)
Bob and Carol and Ted and Alice (1969)
Paper Moon (1973)
Alice Doesn't Live Here Anymore (as *Alice*, 1974)
The Bad News Bears (1976)
Barefoot in the Park (1967)
Mr Deeds Goes to Town (1936)

Ten sitcoms that became movies – but didn't result in three times the fun

Are You Being Served? (1977)
Till Death Us Do Part (1968)
Steptoe and Son (1972)
Dad's Army (1971)
Rising Damp (1980)
The Likely Lads (1976)
Bless This House (1972)
Love Thy Neighbour (1973)
George and Mildred (1980)
Please, Sir (1971)

Jack on the box – Lemmon and Matthau in
The Odd Couple

It's an old cliché, but it might just work – ten Hollywood classics

'Say, why don't we put the show on right here?'
'Wait a minute, boss – the kid can sing'
'Okay, you've got twenty-four hours – then we do it my way'
'All those years searching for happiness and here it was all the time, right under my nose'
'Give me the gun, son, and let's talk about it'
'Promise me you'll tell Mom that I died like a Brewster'
'It's an old trick, but it might just work'
'If I don't come back, will you take care of Jeannie and the kids?'
'And this time nobody's going to stand in my way, not even you'
'I guess I knew all along that it was you she really loved'

'Aren't you on the wrong side of the camera?' Ten directors who've appeared in movies

Steven Spielberg: *The Blues Brothers* (1980)
Martin Scorsese: *Pavlova – A Woman for All Time* (1983)
Lindsay Anderson: *Chariots of Fire* (1981)
François Truffaut: *Close Encounters of the Third Kind* (1977)
John Boorman: *Long Shot* (1978)
Sydney Pollack: *Tootsie* (1982)
Martin Ritt: *The End of the Game* (1976)
Roman Polanski: *Chinatown* (1974)
Preston Sturges: *Star Spangled Rhythm* (1942)
Alan Parker: *The Commitments* (1991)

People who have appeared in movies as themselves

Lord Baden-Powell: *The Woodpigeon Patrol* (1930)
Cecil B. De Mille: *Sunset Boulevard* (1950)
Buffalo Bill Cody: *The Life of Buffalo Bill* (1909)
Dame Marie Rambert: *The Red Shoes* (1948)
Nicholas Parsons: *Mr Jolly Lives Next Door* (1987)
A.J.P. Taylor: *Rockets Galore* (1958)
Lech Walesa: *Man of Iron* (1981)
Jimmy Young: *Otley* (1968)
André Previn: *Pepe* (1960)
Moshe Dayan: *Operation Thunderbolt* (1977)

Ten boxers who've appeared in movies

Joe Louis: *Spirit of Youth* (1938)
Jack Dempsey: *The Prizefighter and the Lady* (1933)
Primo Carnera: *A Kid for Two Farthings* (1955)
Terry Downes: *A Study in Terror* (1965)
Sugar Ray Robinson: *Candy* (1968)
Jersey Joe Walcott: *The Harder They Fall* (1956)
Henry Cooper: *Royal Flash* (1975)
Ken Norton: *Mandingo* (1975)
Joe Frazier: *Rocky* (1977)
Freddie Mills: *Carry On Constable* (1960)

'Ready when you are, Mr De Mille' – other sportsmen who've appeared in movies

Graham Hill: *Caravan to Vaccares* (1975)
Bobby Moore: *Escape to Victory* (1981)
Joe Namath: *C.C. & Company* (1970)
Vijay Amritraj: *Octopussy* (1983)
Stirling Moss: *Casino Royale* (1967)
John McEnroe: *Players* (1979)
Pelé: *Hotshot* (1987)
Arnold Palmer: *Call Me Bwana* (1963)
Jim Laker: *The Final Test* (1953)
Nikki Lauda: *Speed Fever* (1978)

From Truffaut to UFO – *Close Encounters of the Third Kind*

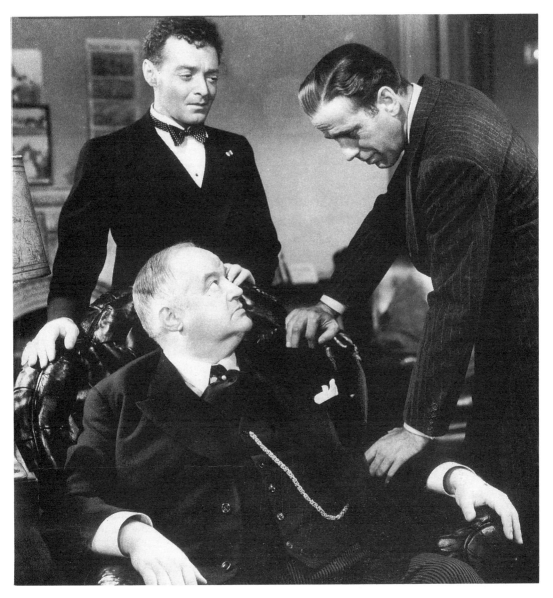

Début smasheroo! Ten stars who started at the top

Jane Russell: *The Outlaw* (1943)
Lauren Bacall: *To Have and Have Not* (1944)
Tatum O'Neal: *Paper Moon* (1973)
Sydney Greenstreet: *The Maltese Falcon* (1941)
Julie Andrews: *Mary Poppins* (1964)
Warren Beatty: *Splendor in the Grass* (1961)
Terence Stamp: *Billy Budd* (1962)
Barbra Streisand: *Funny Girl* (1968)
Orson Welles: *Citizen Kane* (1941)
Kathleen Turner: *Body Heat* (1982)

Play it again, Sydney – Lorre, Greenstreet and Bogart in *The Maltese Falcon*

OFFSCREEN

How to know if you've made it in Hollywood

Your name is romantically linked with Warren Beatty

Robert Redford allows you to call him Bob

Joan Rivers impersonates you on the Johnny Carson show

If Meryl Streep can't do the part, you're definitely next choice

You produce a workout video

Time Out says you've sold out

Your house features on a celebrity bus tour

Your past is uncovered by *The National Enquirer*

You launch your own brand of perfume

You check in at the Betty Ford Clinic

Ten actors who've done time

Stacy Keach: nine months in 1984 for smuggling cocaine

Mae West: eight days in 1927 for taking part in an 'immoral show'

Judy Carne: three months for drug offences in 1986

Phil Silvers: a year in reform school in 1923 for assaulting a teacher

Robert Mitchum: sixty days in 1948 for using marijuana

Ivor Novello: a month in 1944 for breaking wartime defence regulations by driving his Rolls-Royce

Sophia Loren: eighteen days in 1982 for tax evasion

Jane Russell: four days in 1978 for drunk driving

Steve McQueen: sent to reform school for 18 months in 1944 for unruly behaviour

Sean Penn: thirty-three days in 1987 for hitting a film extra

Hollywood's World War II effort

James Stewart was the first major star to sign up (against MGM's wishes). He enlisted as a private in the US Army Air Force and returned to America in September 1945 a Colonel

Cary Grant donated his salary from *The Philadelphia Story* (1940) to war relief

Bette Davis and John Garfield opened the Hollywood Canteen for servicemen in 1942

Clark Gable joined the US Army Air Force (1942)

Myrna Loy worked for the Red Cross in New York and Washington D.C.

Rosalind Russell, Charles Boyer and Cary Grant sold peanuts at a 'Buy a Bomber' Benefit

William Powell donated earnings from a Lux Radio Broadcast to the Red Cross

Robert Montgomery donated an ambulance to the British Red Cross, and went over to England to drive it

David Niven returned to Britain in order to enlist in the Second Battalion – the Rifle Brigade

Leslie Howard was sent, by the British Government, on a secret mission to Spain and Portugal to prevent these countries from joining the Axis Powers

Ten people treated at the Betty Ford Clinic

Elizabeth Taylor
Liza Minnelli
Robert Mitchum
Mary Tyler Moore
Tony Curtis
William Hurt
Chevy Chase
Sean Penn
Richard Pryor
Margaux Hemingway

The marriage merry-go-round –
actresses with husbands in common

Bernadette Peters and Victoria Tennant: Steve
  Martin
Ida Lupino and Joan Fontaine: Collier Young
Elizabeth Taylor and Debbie Reynolds: Eddie
  Fisher
Evelyn Keyes and Ava Gardner: Artie Shaw
Ava Gardner and Mia Farrow: Frank Sinatra
Vivien Leigh and Joan Plowright: Laurence
  Olivier
Mimi Rogers and Nicole Kidman: Tom Cruise
Lana Turner and Arlene Dahl: Lex Barker
Arlene Dahl and Esther Williams: Fernando
  Lamas
Alice Faye and Cyd Charisse: Tony Martin
Kay Kendall and Rachel Roberts: Rex Harrison
Joan Blondell and June Allyson: Dick Powell
Ginger Rogers and Dorothy Malone: Jacques
  Bergerac
Suzy Kendall and Tuesday Weld: Dudley Moore
Jane Wyman and Nancy Davis: Ronald Reagan
Loni Anderson and Judy Carne: Burt Reynolds
Ursula Andress, Linda Evans, Bo Derek: John
  Derek
Anouk Aimée and Jane Wenham: Albert Finney
Barbara Stanwyck and Ursula Thiess: Robert
  Taylor
Lynn Frederick and Britt Ekland: Peter Sellers

Merry-go-round – Frankie goes to Hollywood with
Ava and Mia

Actors with wives in common

William Powell and Clark Gable: Carole Lombard
Michael Wilding and Richard Burton: Elizabeth
  Taylor
Humphrey Bogart and Jason Robards: Lauren
  Bacall
Mickey Rooney and Frank Sinatra: Ava Gardner
Charlie Chaplin and Burgess Meredith: Paulette
  Goddard
Douglas Fairbanks Jr and Franchot Tone: Joan
  Crawford
Ronald Colman and George Sanders: Benita
  Hume
Denholm Elliot and Bill Travers: Virginia
  McKenna
David McCallum and Charles Bronson: Jill Ireland
Lew Ayres and Jacques Bergerac: Ginger Rogers
Jackie Coogan and Harry James: Betty Grable
Jack Hawkins and Hume Cronyn: Jessica Tandy
Don Johnson and Steven Bauer: Melanie Griffith
Richard Greene and Joseph Cotten: Patricia
  Medina
Laurence Harvey and Michael Wilding: Margaret
  Leighton
Maxwell Reed and Anthony Newley: Joan Collins

Hitched twice, trailered many times – Melanie and Don

Ten couples who married each other twice – at least

Don Johnson and Melanie Griffith
Natalie Wood and Robert Wagner
Elizabeth Taylor and Richard Burton
Dorothy Parker and Alan Campbell
Paul Hogan and Noelene Edwards
Elliot Gould and Jenny Bogart
Jane Wyman and Fred Karger
Sarah Miles and Robert Bolt
Hope Lange and Alan J. Pakula
Stan Laurel and Virginia Rogers (three times)

Ten actors who've had novels published

Joan Collins: *Prime Time*
Dirk Bogarde: *West of Sunset*
George Kennedy: *Murder on Location*
David Niven: *Once Over Lightly*
Robert Shaw: *The Man in the Glass Booth*
Anthony Sher: *Middlepost*
Simone Signoret: *Adieu Volodia*
Leslie Caron: *Vengeance*
Diane Cilento: *The Manipulator*
Carrie Fisher: *Postcards from the Edge*

Clint, making Carmel's day

Ten actors who turned to politics

Clint Eastwood: mayor of Carmel
Glenda Jackson: prospective parliamentary
  Labour candidate
Ronald Reagan: president of the US
Melina Mercouri: Greek minister of arts and
  sciences
Sonny Bono: mayor of Palm Springs
Paul Newman: delegate to the 1978 UN
  Conference on Disarmament
John Gavin: US ambassador to Mexico
Vanessa Redgrave: Workers Revolutionary Party
  parliamentary candidate
Shirley Temple: US ambassador to Ghana
Andrew Faulds: Labour MP

MAYOR EASTWOOD

Ten actors who've had hit records

Richard Chamberlain: 'Love Me Tender' (1962)
Richard Harris: 'MacArthur Park' (1968)
Lee Marvin: 'Wand'rin Star' (1970)
Telly Savalas: 'If' (1975)
Edward Woodward: 'The Way You Look Tonight' (1971)
Hayley Mills: 'Let's Get Together' (1961)
Anita Dobson: 'Anyone Can Fall in Love' (1986)
Lorne Greene: 'Ringo' (1964)
Keith Michell: 'I'll Give You the Earth' (1971)
Clint Eastwood: 'I Talk to the Trees' (1970)

Ten actresses who've appeared naked in men's magazines

Madonna
Lesley-Anne Down
Lauren Hutton
Brigitte Bardot
Joan Collins
Lysette Anthony
Ursula Andress
Brigitte Nielsen
Rosanna Arquette
Victoria Principal

Lee Marvin, wand'rin in the bath

Bardot, not always
in the buff

Star-struck – ten couples who fell in love on movie sets

Tom Cruise and Nicole Kidman: *Days of Thunder* (1990)

Richard Burton and Elizabeth Taylor: *Cleopatra* (1963)

William Hurt and Marlee Matlin: *Children of a Lesser God* (1986)

Steve McQueen and Ali MacGraw: *The Getaway* (1972)

Humphrey Bogart and Lauren Bacall: *To Have and Have Not* (1945)

Spencer Tracy and Katharine Hepburn: *Woman of the Year* (1942)

Nicolas Cage and Laura Dern: *Wild at Heart* (1990)

John Malkovich and Michelle Pfeiffer: *Dangerous Liaisons* (1988)

Warren Beatty and Madonna: *Dick Tracy* (1990)

Kiefer Sutherland and Julia Roberts: *Flatliners* (1990)

McQueen and MacGraw getting away from it all

Warning from HM Government – ten actors who advertised cigarettes

Ronald Reagan
Charlton Heston
Lucille Ball
Gregory Peck
Bob Hope
Louis Jordan
Richard Widmark
Marlene Dietrich
Bing Crosby
Joan Crawford

Method madness – things actors have done for movie roles

Robert De Niro gained four stone in weight for *Raging Bull* (1980)

Mariel Hemingway had silicone breast implants for *Star 80* (1983)

Nicholas Cage had two teeth pulled for *Birdy* (1984)

Marlon Brando spent a month in bed to weaken his legs for the role of a paraplegic in *The Men* (1950)

Gary Oldman was treated for malnutrition after starving himself for the part of Sid Vicious in *Sid and Nancy* (1986)

Nick Nolte slaughtered a Borneo pig for *Farewell to the King* (1988)

Charlie Sheen went through a 14-day army training course for *Platoon* (1986)

Michael J. Fox spent three days as a fact-checker on the food pages of *Esquire* magazine for *Bright Lights, Big City* (1988)

Richard Gere lived with Bedouins for *King David* (1985)

Sean Penn stubbed a cigarette out on his palm to 'find' his character as a doped-out surfer in *Fast Times at Ridgemont High* (1982)

Raging Bull – De Niro puts away the punches . . . and the pasta

OUT-TAKES I

Ten movie nightmares

Schwarzenegger's *King Lear*
Robbie Coltrane and Roseanne Barr in *The Postman Always Rings Twice*
Let's Make Love remade as *Let's Take Precautions: The Rock Hudson Story*
A Colin Moynihan bio-pic (*The Mickey Rooney Tory*)
Apocalypse Now remade as a musical (*Apocalypso Now*)
The Silence of the Lambs 2 (*Afters*)
Ken Russell remakes *The Sound of Music* starring Madonna
Alastair Sim, Margaret Rutherford and Robert Morley in *Naked as Nature Intended*
101 Pit Bull Terriers

The ten unknown Marx Brothers

Garbo Marx: the reclusive brother who was occasionally spotted in supermarkets
Bronco Marx: the sickly brother who was a martyr to diarrhoea all his life
Rambo Marx: the muscle-bound brother with a speech impediment
Dumbo Marx: the deaf-mute brother who taught Harpo all he knew
Sumo Marx: the incontinent brother who was forced to wear giant nappies
Robbo Marx: the sporting brother who was always injured
Bimbo Marx: the transvestite brother who was banned by the Hays Office
Psycho Marx: the wild-eyed brother with a shower fetish
Sambo Marx: the token non-white brother
Brando Marx: the brooding brother who always believed he could have been a contender

Ten movie sequels we're waiting for

Willy Wonka and the Dental Appointment
The Postgraduate
Babette's Washing-Up
Saturday the 14th
The Retirement of Duddy Kravitz
Total Memory Loss
Three Men and a Teenager
Sunday Night and Monday Morning
Conditioner
The Postman Always Pushes A Card Through The Door Asking You To Go Down To The Sorting Office

Ten movie 'prequels' we're waiting for

Thursday the 12th
Undercoat Your Wagon
The Draughtsman's Estimate
Daydream on Elm Street
Friday Night and Saturday Morning
The Undergraduate
The Catering Student, the Juvenile Offender, His Girlfriend, and Her Chum
Guess Who's Coming to Tea?
Kramer Marries Kramer
The Godson Part One

Ten predictions for 2010

Zsa Zsa Gabor and Mickey Rooney finally get
    round to each other
A new book of Marilyn Monroe photographs
Michael Jackson is completely rebuilt
The Betty Ford Clinic takes over Hollywood
George Burns in *Oh, Methuselah*
President Schwarzenegger
A Robin Askwith retrospective at the NFT
Posthumous Academy Award for Steven Spielberg
    (he dies of shock when his name is read out)
Seriously Overage Mutant Ninja Turtles
Stallone speaks!

Mad movie clips

'Darling, I've got two tickets for the Beckett
    season at the National Theatre' (*Misery*)
'I could murder a bowl of cornflakes' (*Henry:
    Portrait of a Serial Killer*)
'Ooh, shut that door!' (*Backdraft*)
'Let me out of here, I can't stand crowds' (*In Bed
    with Madonna*)
'Allan said nothing about being dropped, and
    neither did his wife' (*The Silence of the Lambs*)
'That's my two hundreth application, and still no
    job' (*The Graduate*)
'Hello, I'm Victor Ki . . . aagh!' (*Death of a
    Salesman*)
'Dear Bono, having a wonderful time, wish you
    were here' (*Postcards from The Edge*)
'I knew I shouldn't have had that curry' (*Gone
    With The Wind*)
'I don't care what anybody says, I raise my glass to
    Jeremy Beadle' (*The Brave Little Toaster*)

Ten classic Hollywood medical conditions

Casting-couch potato's bottom
Cirrhosis of the loose-liver
Designer stubble abrasions
Silicone fatigue
Psychiatrist's wallet-strain
Palimonic depression
Chronic taste deficiency
Scarlet O'Hara fever
Single-earringworm
Grauman's Chinese cement burns

Due to open in 2010 – Rambo's mouth

Movie career on the slide? Ten tell-tale signs

Your agent goes ex-Directory
You can't afford your drink problem
BBC2 runs a season of your films
You start chasing the paparazzi
You do guest spots on *Sesame Street*
Your Grauman's Chinese handprints are cemented
    over to accommodate a Teenage Mutant Ninja
    Turtle
Your analyst pronounces you cured
You run for president
Critics refer to your films as cult movies
You're elected president

Cagney, Public Enemy with the grapefruit touch

Relationship on the rocks, Hollywoodstyle? Ten tell-tale signs for the wife

He signs up to do a film with Julia Roberts
He cancels your subscription to *The National Enquirer*
You find palimony calculations in his pocket
He gets into the habit of dropping into Dr Ruth's gym most nights for a workout
Madonna starts auditioning for her next lover
He insists on separate analysts
He introduces you to Warren Beatty
He pushes a half grapefruit into your face
He has the locks changed while you're nude sunbathing
He moves into the spare room – at his lawyer's house

Reviving the British movie industry – ten remakes to get us going

The Mancunian Candidate
Meet Me in St Alban's
The Bridge on the River Wye
Bad Day at Blackpool Rock
The Life and Times of Judge James Pickles
Our Man in Havant
Ron Brown's Schooldays
Song of Norwood
The Greatest Tory Ever Sold
All Quiet on the Western Bypass

Ten movies for football fans

The Groom Wore Spurs (1951)
The Petrified Forest (1936)
Villa Rides (1968)
The City (1939)
The Texas Rangers (1936)
Reds (1981)
The Sea Wolves (1980)
Kind Hearts and Coronets (1949)
The Arsenal Stadium Mystery (1939)
Dances with Wolves (1991)

Ten dishes from the Hannibal Lecter cookbook

Toe-in-the-hole
Donor kebab
Cornish Patsy
Patella *de foie gras*
Crocked monsieur
Shepherd pie
Dover soul
Chilian con carne
Boiled Swedes
Sour Kraut

Where Hollywood meets Fleet Street

The Guardian (1984)
Von Ryan's Express (1965)
Crack in the Mirror (1960)
The Man Without a Star (1955)
Mail Order Bride (1963)
Hard Times (1975)
People on Sunday (1929)
Greed in the Sun (1964)
Foreign Correspondent (1940)
The Single Standard (1929)

Ten movie remakes for the 1990s

A Fistful of ECUs
How Green Was My Manifesto
Above Us the Raw Sewage
Reach for the Hole in the Ozone Layer
The Community Charge of the Light Brigade
War and Greenpeace
Invasion of the Liver and Kidney Snatchers
Centigrade 232
Maggie – A Suitable Case for Treatment
Around the M25 in 80 Days

Ten *Indiana Jones* movies still on the drawing board

Indiana Jones and the Last Bus to Barnsley
Indiana Jones and the Missing Pink Frock
*Indiana Jones and the Cordon Bleu Cookery
    Course*
Indiana Jones and the Multiple Share Application
Indiana Jones and the Wife's Mother's Hat
Indiana Jones and the Winning Premium Bond
Indiana Jones and the Seven-Day Diet
*Indiana Jones and the Weekend Shopping
    Expedition*
Indiana Jones and the Unfortunate Haircut
Indiana Jones and the Self-Catering Holiday

Anyone for dinner? Hannibal the Cannibal

Ten biblical epics waiting to be made

Return of the Magi
Play it Again, Samaritan
The Night They Raided Gethsemane's
Palm Sunday, Bloody Palm Sunday
Man of La Manger
Three Wise Men and A Baby
The Promised Land or Bust
The Cain Mutiny
Lazarus Has Risen From the Grave
Guess Who's Coming to Supper

Ten movies for chocoholics

Mutiny on the Bounty (1935)
The Milky Way (1936)
Marathon Man (1976)
Galaxy of Terror (1981)
The Penguin Pool Murder (1932)
Taxi Driver (1976)
Picnic at Hanging Rock (1975)
The Lady and the Bandit (1951)
Trio (1950)
Invaders from Mars (1953)

Those BAFTA awards – ten new categories

Best use of Michael Caine
Best performance in an Australian soap opera, excluding furniture
The Baron Munchausen Memorial Award for going most over budget
Most convincing use of canned laughter
Best best-boy
Most spectacular use of expenses on a holiday programme
Best game show in the 'Under £300 Per Programme' category
Best film with the word 'fish' in the title
Lifetime achievement award for never having previously won an award

Ten productions for ham actors

The Days of Swine and Roses
Porky and Bess
From Rasher with Love
All Quiet on the Western Runt
Barefoot in the Pork
The Old Curiosity Chop
The Pig Sleep
The Hogs of War
Lord of the Pies
Pigmalion

Ten selections from our movie critic

The Four Horsemen of the Apocalypse and a Baby
Nightmare on Network South-East
House of Commons Researcher on the Job
Three Rain Men and a Baby
Rimbaud 3
The Long Good Friday 13th, Part Two
A Haddock called Wanda
Who Framed the Mona Lisa?
The Sound of Muzak
Three Gorillas in the Mist and a Chimpanzee

A fruit salad of movies

The Greengage Summer (1961)
Wild Strawberries (1957)
A Clockwork Orange (1971)
Bananas (1971)
The Apple Dumpling Gang (1974)
Watermelon Man (1970)
Eat the Peach (1986)
Can She Bake a Cherry Pie? (1983)
The Lemon-Drop Kid (1951)
The Grapes of Wrath (1940)

Soft soap – Michael Caine cleans up for BAFTA

Ten stages in the making of a movie

Lunch
Idea
Treatment
Script
Pre-production
Filming
Post-production
Hype
Written off against tax as a flop
Lunch

Being a Royal is just like acting

Ten commandments for actors

Thou shalt have no other gods before thee

Thou shalt not make unto thee any graven image-maker who is not recommended by the studio

Thou shalt not take the name of the Lord thy Grade in vain

Remember the rest day in thy contract and keep it holy that thou might network efficiently

Honour thy father and mother when thou receives an Academy Award

Thou shalt not commit adultery but multiple marriages will not a career harm

Thou shalt not steal a scene – yea, verily even if thou art up against a total ham

Thou shalt not bear false witness against thy latest release when being interviewed by Johnny Carson

Thou shalt not covet a role in a soap opera lest thou be cast out from the Hollywood firmament

Thou shalt not kill for a better trailer for why else did God invent agents

'And that's me, fourth row second from left'

Actor-speak – a guide to interpretation

'Acting's just a job': *Like being a member of the Royal Family is*

'I don't believe in awards': *I wasn't even nominated*

'I've just finished doing Hamlet': *I've just done a TV commercial for cigars*

'Of course, theatre is my first love': *This tour of North Yorkshire was all my agent could get me*

'When Larry and I were on stage together': *I was the one carrying the spear*

'I'm resting': *I'm unemployed*

'I'm unemployed': *I'm unemployable*

'I suppose actors are children who never grew up': *That's why I throw tantrums all the time*

'It's very much the writer's film': *I couldn't understand a word of it*

'I never read the critics': *They never write about me*

Orson Welles, the thin man waiting to get out

Ten sponsored movies

Dewhurst's *The Silence of the Lambs*
EXIT's *No Way Out*
Dateline's *When Harry Met Sally*
Mothercare's *She's Having a Baby*
Panadol's *Dr No*
Benson & Hedges' *Hamlet*
Thomas Cook's *If It's Tuesday, This Must Be Belgium*
Duracell's *Batteries Not Included*
Sony's *Radio Days*
Citroën's *The Cars That Ate Paris*

The movies they should've made

Kirk and Michael Douglas: *Dimples* (1936)
Timothy Bottoms: *Hallelujah I'm a Bum* (1933)
Peter Finch and Walter Pigeon: *The Birds* (1963)
Tatum O'Neal: *Ryan's Daughter* (1970)
Liz Taylor: *The Battle of the Bulge* (1965)
Harpo Marx: *The Quiet Man* (1952)
Boy George: *Georgy Girl* (1966)
Orson Welles: *After the Thin Man* (1936)
Dolly Parton: *Hollywood or Bust* (1956)
Bobby and Lucille Ball: *Screwballs* (1983)

Green movies – ten movies for gardeners

Back to the Fuschia
101 Carnations
The Land that Thyme Forgot
Plantasia
The Cruel Seed
Butch Cassidy and the Sunflower Kid
A Fistful of Dahlias
The Magnificent Sedum
The Longest Daisy
The Germinator

How Bergmanesque! A guide to serious movie crits

'An erotic comedy of manners': *Socially acceptable skinflick*
'Loosely-woven narrative structure': *No plot*
'Ends on an enigmatic note': *Impossible to work out who did it*
'Full of raw energy': *They didn't edit it*
'Imbued with moral uncertainties': *Hero sleeps with all the women*
'Notable for its chromatic dichotomy': *Bits are in black and white*
'Self-referential': *Rambo XII*
'Recently reappraised': *You can now admit to liking it*
'Cinéma vérité': *Shaky camera*
'Confirms the emergence of Third World cinema': *Subtitled*

Ten principal causes of divorce in Hollywood

Irreconcilable differences (for example, male/female)
Even chance of getting shot of the kids
The best alimony rates in the world
Lawyers on a percentage
Good private detectives
Certainty of getting rid of the mother-in-law
Giggling during spouse's love scenes at film premières
Oprah Winfrey Show
Changing channels during sex
Changing partners during sex

Kevin Costner, unlikely to cha-cha with corgis

Ten movie projects that might not make it into production

Mel Gibson in *Hamlet II*
Have I the Right, an Oliver Stone biopic of The Honeycombs' drummer
Three Men and an Old-Age Pensioner
Gérard Depardieu as Réné in a big screen version of *'Allo 'Allo*
The true story of the Celtic tribes, *Dances with Corgis*
Star Trek 12: The Search for Scotty's Waistline
A remake of *The Greatest Story Ever Told*, starring David Icke
Awakenings II, featuring the entire House of Lords
Jason and Kylie in *The Tracy and Hepburn Story*
Terminator III – The Musical

Arnie's ambition is just to keep working

Ten lines all actors learn at drama school

'One's so lucky to be paid for doing something one would do for nothing'

'Get the walk right and the rest of the character follows'

'Comedy's so much harder to do than the straight stuff'

'Of course, it always comes back to that playwright from Stratford'

'My ambition is just to keep working'

'Nothing matches live theatre for getting the adrenalin going'

'I was always mimicking the teachers at school, as a kind of defence mechanism I suppose'

'Awards are nice, but they're not what the business is all about'

'I think one learns to live with the insecurity – and be grateful for the times when one is in work'

'It may seem glamorous, but there's an awful lot of hanging around when you do film work'

Ten movies for a recession

Debt in Venice
The King and IOU
Penny from Heaven
The Loan Arranger
Begging Letter to Brezhnev
The Owed Curiosity Shop
A Comedy of Arrears
Hock around the Clock
Bill de Jour
This Gun for Hire Purchase

Ten movie partnerships we're waiting for

Paul Newman and Gary Oldman
Randolph Scott and Raquel Welch
Jim Brown and Barbara Windsor
Roger Moore and Anton Lesser
Edward Fox and Gareth Hunt
George Brent and Ben Cross
Lorne Greene and Clark Gable
Winona Ryder and Clint Walker
Elke Sommer and Shelley Winters
Jeremy Irons and Tuesday Weld

Ten movies you can grow in your garden

Goldfinger (Mexican sunflower), 1964
African Queen (Lily), 1951
Bright Eyes (Primula), 1934
Summer Holiday (Rose), 1962
Peter Pan (Zinnia), 1953
Showboat (Marigold), 1936
Paper Moon (Scabious), 1973
Pinocchio (Aster), 1940
Casablanca (Delphinium), 1942
Cinderella (Snapdragon), 1950

Ten movies for Oliver Reed to star in

Close Encounters of the Blurred Kind
For Whom the Bell's Tolls
The Booze Brothers
Billy Buddweiser
Romancing the Stone's
The Best Beers of Our Lives
The 39 Schnapps
My Brilliant Careering
Honey, I Drunk the Gins
Double Diamonds are Forever

The pervert's movie guide
Full Rubber Jacket
Bob and Carol and Ted and Fido
The Thong of Norway
Gentlemen Prefer Bonds
Those Magnificent Men in Their Flaying Machines
The Man Who Would Be Queen
The Dirty Dozen Raincoats
The John Thomas Crown Affair
Goodbye, Mr Whips
The Man in the Iron Basque

Ten movies for the under-fives
The Pink Pamper
Infantasia
Ring of Gripe Water
High Chair Society
Postman Pat Always Rings Twice
Young Gums
I was Monty's Dribble
Nightmare on Sesame Street
Prambo
The Crèche from the Black Lagoon

Movies for the faint-hearted
Conan the Librarian
Everything You Always Wanted to Know About
* Socks (But Were Afraid to Ask)*
The Mild Bunch
The Texas Chainstore Massacre
Bob and Carol and Darby and Joan
Invasion of the Body Scratchers
Robochef
A Man Called Horace
9½ Leeks
Dial M for Maidstone

Ten movies for royal premières
The Man Who Fell to Earth (Prince Charles) 1976
Charley's Aunt (Princess Margaret) 1941
Outrageous Fortune (The Queen) 1986
Rancho Deluxe (The Duke of York) 1974
Bringing Up Baby (The Duchess of York) 1938
The Trouble with Harry (Prince William) 1955
The Good Companions (The Princess Royal and
  Timothy Laurence) 1956
It's a Wonderful Life (The Queen Mother) 1946
The Prince and the Pauper (Prince Michael of
  Kent) 1977
The Wild One (Prince Edward) 1954

Dr Strangelove: slim pickings for Neil Kinnock?

A selection of movies for politicians
Neil Kinnock: *Dr Strangelove: Or How I Learned
  to Stop Worrying and Love The Bomb* (1963)
Robert Maclennan: *The Man Who Never Was*
  (1955)
John Major: *The Man in Grey* (1943)
Cecil Parkinson: *Parenthood* (1989)
Ted Heath: *Rebel Without a Cause* (1955)
James Callaghan: *Lord Jim* (1964)
Colin Moynihan: *The Incredible Shrinking Man*
  (1957)
Roy Hattersley: *Guess Who's Coming to Dinner*
  (1967)
David Owen: *Dr No* (1962)
Any member of the SDP: *And Then There Were
  None* (1974)

Ten casting ideas that never got off the ground

Woody Allen as Conan the Barbarian
Penelope Keith as Annie Hall
Julie Andrews as Emmanuelle
Spike Milligan as James Bond
Ronnie Corbett as Robocop
Paul Eddington as Dirty Harry
Julie Walters as Alexis Carrington
Joan Collins as Snow White
Little and Large as Butch Cassidy and the
    Sundance Kid
Julian Clary as Rambo

Grounded: Woody muscles up as Conan the Barbarian

Ten movies for sports stars

Nick Faldo: *Drive He Said* (1970)
Carl Lewis: *Black Narcissus* (1946)
Nigel Mansell: *Outrageous Fortune* (1986)
Paul Gascoigne: *How to Get Ahead in Advertising*
    (1988)
Allan Border: *The Wizard of Oz* (1939)
John McEnroe: *Bringing Up Baby* (1938)
Desmond Lynam: *A Man For All Seasons* (1966)
Graham Gooch: *Superman* (1978)
André Agassi: *Hair* (1979)
Mike Tyson: *The Terminator* (1984)

Ten movies for cricket lovers
The Third Man (1949)
Fletch (1985)
The Final Test (1953)
Hello Dolly (1969)
Ashes and Diamonds (1958)
Over Twenty-One (1945)
Point Blank (1967)
Captain Boycott (1947)
Hook (1991)
State of Grace (1991)

Ten great wooden performances
The Log Lady's log in *Twin Peaks* (1989)
The vaulting horse in *The Wooden Horse* (1950)
Long John Silver's crutch in *Treasure Island* (1934)
The bridge in *The Bridge on the River Kwai* (1957)
The Trojan horse in *Helen of Troy* (1955)
The scenery in *Neighbours* (1986–)
Sherwood Forest in *The Adventures of Robin Hood* (1938)
Al Capone's baseball bat in *The Untouchables* (1987)
The ship in *Mutiny on the Bounty* (1962)
The raft in *How the West was Won* (1962)

Ten movies they shouldn't show on an aeroplane
No Escape (1936)
Lost Horizon (1937)
The Crash (1932)
Terror Aboard (1933)
The Flight That Disappeared (1961)
Skyjacked (1972)
No Highway (1951)
Storm Warning (1950)
Broken Journey (1948)
The Flight of the Phoenix (1965)

Ten films to whet the appetite
In Bed With Ma Dinner
Night of the Living Bread
A Man for all Seasonings
Romancing the Scone
The Magnificent Seven-Up
Hot-Dog Day Afternoon
The Long Good Fried Egg
His Grill Friday
The Fridge on the River Kwai
The Gruellists

Anthony Perkins, no shower-gel salesman

Ten merchandising spin-offs that never really caught on
Silence of the Lambs pâté
Last Tango in Paris butter (very salty)
Poseidon Adventure cruises
Psycho shower-gel
Fatal Attraction dating agency
(Laurel & Hardy) *Another Fine Mess* disposable nappies
Lost Weekend vodka
Mutiny On The Bounty bars
Backdraft firelighters
Freddie fishfingers

The Long Good Friday: Bob Hoskins, Helen Mirren and Eddie Constantine toast the rest of the week

Something for the weekend? Ten movies to watch on a Saturday

Saturday Island (1951)
Saturday Night and Sunday Morning (1960)
Saturday Night at the Baths (1974)
Saturday Night Fever (1978)
Saturday the 14th (1981)
Saturday's Children (1940)
Saturday the 14th Strikes Back (1988)
Saturday's Hero (1951)
Saturday Night at the Palace (1988)
Saturday Night Out (1963)

Ten movies to watch for the rest of the week

Never on Sunday (1959)
Stormy Monday (1987)
If It's Tuesday, This Must Be Belgium (1969)
Ash Wednesday (1973)
Thursday's Child (1942)
Man Friday (1975)
Freaky Friday (1976)
Thank God It's Friday (1978)
The Long Good Friday (1980)
Friday the Thirteenth (1980)

QUOTATIONS

Actors talking about their favourite subject – themselves

Alan Ladd: 'I have the face of an ageing choirboy and the build of an undernourished featherweight. If you can figure out my success on the screen you're a better man than I'

Greta Garbo: 'I'm not a versatile actress'

Groucho Marx: 'If you want to see a comic strip, you should see me in a shower'

James Stewart: 'I don't act. I react'

Burt Lancaster: 'I'm bookish and worrisome'

Marilyn Monroe: 'I seem to be a whole superstructure with no foundation'

Clark Gable: 'I'm no actor and never have been. What people see on the stage is me'

Mickey Rooney: 'I was a fourteen-year-old boy for twenty years'

Charlie Chaplin: 'I remain one thing and one thing only, and that's a clown. It places me on a far higher plane than any politician'

John Wayne: 'I play John Wayne in every part regardless of character'

Big Leggy plays himself

Horray for Hollywood!

'Hollywood is the only place where an amicable divorce means each one gets 50 per cent of the publicity' (Lauren Bacall)

'In Hollywood, if a guy's wife looks like a new woman, she probably is' (Dean Martin)

'Hollywood: where people from Iowa mistake each other for movie stars' (Fred Allen)

'Hollywood's the place where they'll pay you a thousand dollars for a kiss and 50 cents for your soul' (Marilyn Monroe)

'Hollywood is where, if you don't have happiness, you send out for it' (Rex Reed)

'A place where they shoot too many pictures and not enough actors' (Walter Winchell)

'Hollywood is a strange place when you're in trouble. Everyone is afraid it's contagious' (Judy Garland)

'Hollywood is a sewer, with service from the Ritz-Carlton' (Wilson Mizner)

'They only know one word of more than one syllable here, and that is fillum' (Louis Sherwin)

'In Europe an actor is an artist. In Hollywood, if he isn't acting, he's a bum' (Anthony Quinn)

Ten Woody Allen one-liners

'I don't want to achieve immortality through my work. I want to achieve it through not dying'

'The lion and the calf shall lie down together, but the calf won't get much sleep'

'Money is better than poverty, if only for financial reasons'

'It's not that I'm afraid to die – I just don't want to be there when it happens'

'Sex between a man and a woman can be wonderful – provided you get between the right man and the right woman'

'Not only is there no God, but try getting a plumber on weekends'

'My brain: it's my second favourite organ'

'Is sex dirty? Only if it's done right'

'My one regret in life is that I'm not someone else'

'Life is hard, and then you die'

Ten Groucho Marx one-liners

'Groucho isn't my real name – I'm breaking it in for a friend'

'I never forget a face, but in your case I'll make an exception'

'My mother loved children – she would have given anything if I'd been one'

'I eat like a vulture – unfortunately, the resemblance doesn't end there'

'This would be a better world for children if parents had to eat the spinach'

'Behind every successful screenwriter stands a woman – and behind her stands his wife'

'I've been around so long I knew Doris Day before she was a virgin'

'Only one man in a thousand is a leader of men – the other 999 follow women'

'Go, and never darken my towels again!'

'I don't want to belong to any club that would have me as a member'

The $1,000 kiss – Gable and Monroe in *The Misfits*

Bacall and Bogart – 100 per cent of the publicity and *no* divorce

'Keep cool and collect' – Mae West and W.C. Fields in *My Little Chickadee*

Ten Mae West one-liners

'Keep a diary and one day it will keep you'

'I used to be Snow White, but I drifted'

'Marriage is a great institution, but I'm not ready for an institution yet'

'Keep cool and collect'

'She's the kind of girl who climbed the ladder of success, wrong by wrong'

'A man in the house is worth two in the street'

'I'm the girl who lost her reputation, but never missed it'

'Some women pick men to marry: others pick them to pieces'

'Virtue has its own reward, but no sale at the box office'

'Whenever I'm caught between two evils, I take the one I've never tried'

Going Zsa Zsa – ten quotes from Ms Gabor

'You never really know a man until you've divorced him'

'I want a man who's kind and understanding – is that too much to ask of a millionaire?'

'I believe in large families: every woman should have at least three husbands'

'I never really hated a man enough to give him his diamonds back'

'I'm a marvellous housekeeper – every time I leave a man I keep his house'

'Getting divorced just because you don't love a man is almost as silly as getting married just because you love him'

'The only place men want depth in a woman is in her *décolletage*'

'The women's movement hasn't changed my sex life at all: it wouldn't dare'

'If they had as much adultery going on in New York as they said in the divorce courts, they would never have a chance to make the beds at the Plaza'

'You mean apart from my own?' (when asked how many husbands she'd had)

Errol Flynn, swashbuckling against good taste

Ten put-downs

'Bogart's a helluva nice guy till 10.30 p.m. After that he thinks he's Bogart' (David Chasen)

'Surely no one but a mother could have loved Bette Davis at the height of her career' (Brian Aherne)

'His main purpose seemed to be to break as many rules as possible and cause the maximum amount of trouble for everybody' (Robert Lewis Taylor, of W.C. Fields)

'His life was a fifty year trespass against good taste' (Leslie Mallory, of Errol Flynn)

'Clark is the sort of guy, if you say "Hiya Clark, how are ya?" – he's stuck for an answer' (Ava Gardner, of Clark Gable)

'Kissing her is like kissing Hitler' (Tony Curtis, of Marilyn Monroe)

'He sounds like he has a mouth full of wet toilet paper' (Rex Reed, of Marlon Brando)

'She ran the gamut of the emotions from A to B' (Dorothy Parker, on Katharine Hepburn)

'He has a face that convinces you that God is a cartoonist' (Jack Kroll, of Woody Allen)

'Working with her is like being hit over the head with a Valentine's card' (Christopher Plummer, of Julie Andrews)

Ten quotes about actors, darling

'An actor is a guy who, if you aren't talking about him, isn't listening' (Marlon Brando)

'I didn't say "actors are like cattle". I said "actors should be treated like cattle"' (Alfred Hitchcock)

'A fan club is a group of people who tell an actor he is not alone in the way he feels about himself' (Jack Carson)

'All actors are darlings backstage' (Bamber Gascoigne)

'Some of the greatest love affairs I've known involved one actor, unassisted' (Wilson Mizner)

'You can pick out the actors by the glazed look that comes into their eyes when the conversation wanders away from themselves' (Michael Wilding)

'Actors and burglars work better at night' (Sir Cedric Hardwicke)

'Very good actors never talk about their art. Very bad ones never stop' (John Whiting)

'Most actresses just read their own lines to find out what clothes they're going to wear' (Anita Loos)

'The best screen actor is that man who can do nothing extremely well' (Alfred Hitchcock)

Marlon, not listening

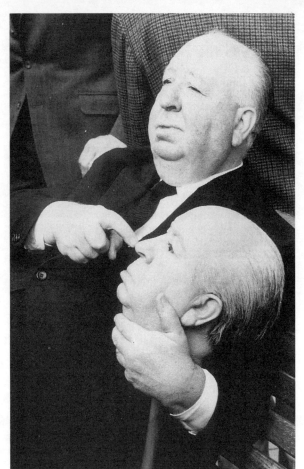

Hitchcock, twice thirty-five and still ahead, ho ho

By George – ten George Burns quotes

'I can remember when the air was clean and sex was dirty'

'When I was a young man, the Dead Sea was still alive'

'Whenever I complain that things aren't what they used to be, I always forget to include myself'

'I have my eighty-seventh birthday coming up and people ask what I'd most appreciate getting. I'll tell you: a paternity suit'

'With the collapse of vaudeville new talent has no place to stink'

'I smoke ten to fifteen cigars a day – at my age I have to hold on to something'

'Acting is all about honesty. If you can fake that, you've got it made'

'Too bad all the people who know how to run the country are busy driving taxi cabs and cutting hair'

'Retirement at sixty-five is ridiculous. When I was sixty-five I still had pimples'

'Actually, it only takes one drink to get me loaded. Trouble is I can't remember if it's the thirteenth or fourteenth'

Ten Harpo Marx one-liners

- •
- •
- •
- •
- •
- •
- •
- •
- •
- •

And it's • • • • • from h

Ten Alfred Hitchcock quotes

'When people say I'm seventy I say that's a confounded lie. I'm twice thirty-five, that's all. Twice thirty-five'

'Drama is life with the dull bits cut out'

'A good film is when the price of the dinner, the theatre admission and the babysitter were worth it'

'The chief requisite of an actor is the ability to do nothing well, which is by no means so easy as it seems'

'The length of a film should be directly related to the endurance of the human bladder'

'Never judge a country by its politics. After all, we English are quite honest by nature, aren't we?'

'The cinema is not a slice of life but a piece of cake'

'If I made *Cinderella* the audience would be looking out for a body in the coach'

'Conversation is the enemy of good wine and food'

'There is no terror in a bang, only in the anticipation of it'

Ten Mel Brooks quotes

'Critics can't even make music by rubbing their back legs together'

'If presidents don't do it to their wives, they do it to the country'

'These people are simple farmers, people of the land, the common clay of the New West. You know – morons'

'There's a sexual revolution going on, and I think that with our current foreign policy, we'll probably be sending troops in there any minute to break it up'

'Usually, when a lot of men get together, it's called war'

'Bad taste is simply saying the truth before it should be said'

'Tragedy is if I cut my finger. Comedy is if I walk into an open sewer and die'

'That's it, baby. If you've got it, flaunt it'

'God is like a Jewish waiter, he has too many tables'

'You are always a little disappointing in person because you can't be the edited essence of yourself'

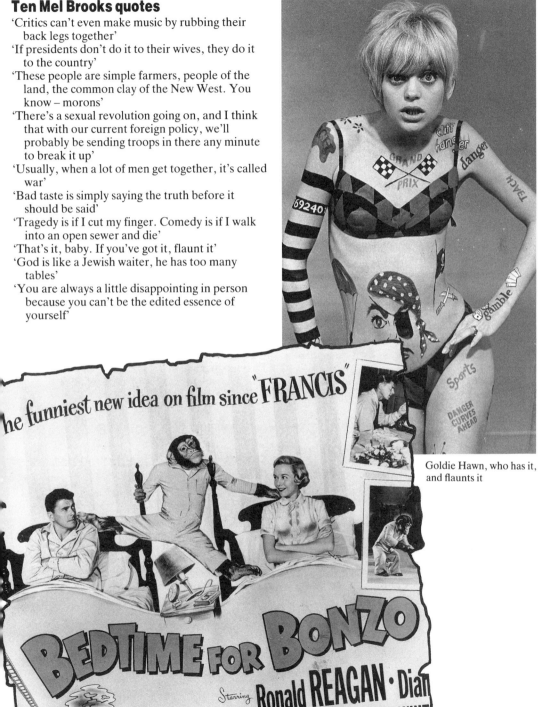

Goldie Hawn, who has it, and flaunts it

Ronnie, doing it to the cinema before the country

FOR THE RECORD

Plum parts actors have turned down

Robert Redford: Dustin Hoffman's role in *The Graduate* (1967)

Henry Fonda: Peter Finch's Oscar-winning role in *Network* (1976)

Humphrey Bogart: James Mason's role in *A Star is Born* (1954)

Audrey Hepburn: Millie Perkins' title role in *The Diary of Anne Frank* (1959)

Eddie Cantor: Al Jolson's role in *The Jazz Singer* (1927)

Lee Marvin: George C. Scott's Oscar-winning role as *Patton* (1970)

Norma Shearer: Greer Garson's Oscar-winning performance in the title role of *Mrs Miniver* (1942)

Marlon Brando: Robert Redford's Sundance in *Butch Cassidy and The Sundance Kid* (1969)

George Raft: Humphrey Bogart's Sam Spade in *The Maltese Falcon* (1941)

Vanessa Redgrave: Lynn Redgrave's role as *Georgy Girl* (1966)

Ten movie directors who started off making commercials

Adrian Lyne (*Fatal Attraction*): Fiat Strada

Alan Parker (*Fame*): Birds' Eye Beefburgers

Hugh Hudson (*Chariots of Fire*): Cinzano

Ridley Scott (*Alien*): Hovis

Mike Hodges (*A Prayer for the Dying*): Cadbury's Milk Tray

Tony Scott (*Top Gun*): Saab

Mike Radford (*White Mischief*): Top Man

Richard Loncraine (*Bellman & True*): British Airways

Paul Weiland (*Leonard Part 6*): Heineken

Mike Newell (*Dance with a Stranger*): COI

Ten movie firsts

First movie without a single subtitle (all the credits are spoken): *The Terror* (1928)

First movie made in Hollywood: *In Old California* (1910)

First talking picture made in Hollywood: *They're Coming to Get Me* (1926)

First Western: *Arizona* (1913)

First musical with original score: *The Broadway Melody* (1929)

First all-talking feature film: *Lights of New York* (1928)

First talkie made in Britain: *Blackmail* (1929)

First British musical: *Raise the Roof* (1930)

First Cinemascope film: *The Robe* (1953)

First child to earn a million dollars in films (or any other business): Jackie Coogan (1914–84)

The ten greatest disaster movies (financially, that is)

The Adventures of Baron Munchausen (1988) lost $48.1m

Ishtar (1987) lost $47.3m

Inchon (1981) lost $44.1m

The Cotton Club (1984) lost $38.1m

Santa Claus: The Movie (1985) lost $37m

Heaven's Gate (1980) lost $34.2m

Pirates (1986) lost $30.3m

Rambo III (1988) lost $30m

Raise The Titanic (1980) lost $29.2m

Revolution (1985) lost $27m

E.T. – we're talking telephone numbers

The biggest box-office successes of the past decade in the UK

Arthur (1982)
E.T. (1983)
Indiana Jones and The Temple of Doom (1984)
Ghostbusters (1985)
Back to the Future (1986)
Crocodile Dundee (1987)
Fatal Attraction (1988)
Indiana Jones and The Last Crusade (1989)
Ghost (1990)
Robin Hood: Prince of Thieves (1991)

If at first you don't succeed . . . Clint Eastwood's first ten movies

Revenge of the Creature (1955)
Francis in the Navy (1955)
Lady Godiva (1955)
Tarantula! (1956)
Never Say Goodbye (1956)
Star in the Dust (1956)
The First Travelling Saleslady (1956)
Escapade in Japan (1957)
Lafayette Escadrille (1957)
Ambush at Cimarron Pass (1958)
(No 11 was *A Fistful of Dollars* in 1964)

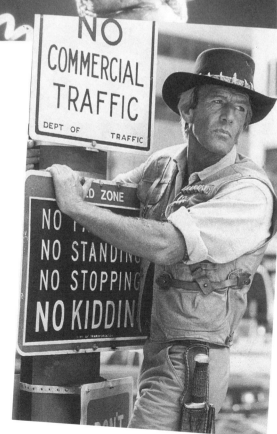

No kidding, mate, the cheque's in the post

The British Film Institute's ten greatest movies of all time

Casablanca (1942)
Les Enfants du Paradis (1943–5)
Citizen Kane (1941)
Singin' in the Rain (1952)
2001: A Space Odyssey (1968)
Some Like it Hot (1959)
Seven Samurai (1954)
Gone with the Wind (1939)
The Third Man (1949)
One Flew over the Cuckoo's Nest (1975)

Ten more plum parts actors have turned down

W.C. Fields: the title role in *The Wizard of Oz* (1939)
Alan Ladd: James Dean's role in *Giant* (1956)
Kirk Douglas: Lee Marvin's Oscar-winning Kid Sheleen in *Cat Ballou* (1965)
Bette Davis: Scarlett O'Hara in *Gone with the Wind* (1939)
Burt Lancaster: the lead in *Ben-Hur* (1959)
Hedy Lamarr: Ingrid Bergman's Ilse in *Casablanca* (1942)
William Holden: Gregory Peck's role in *The Guns of Navarone* (1961)
Jane Fonda: Bonnie Parker in *Bonnie and Clyde* (1967)
Montgomery Clift: William Holden's role in *Sunset Boulevard* (1950)
George Raft: Humphrey Bogart's role in *Casablanca* (1942)

Jack Nicholson, as cuckoo as they come

It never did me any harm – Jeremy Irons

Ten actors who went to public school

Terry-Thomas: Ardingly
George Sanders: Brighton College
Nigel Davenport: Cheltenham College
Rupert Everett: Ampleforth
Michael Redgrave: Clifton
Simon MacCorkindale: Haileybury
Robin Ellis: Highgate
Robert Hardy: Rugby
Jeremy Irons: Sherborne
David Tomlinson: Tonbridge

Cut! Ten movies that were banned

Sophie's Choice (1982) was banned in Syria because 'it aroused sympathy with Jews'
The Grapes of Wrath (1940) was banned in the USSR because it showed that however poor Americans were, they could still afford a car
All Quiet on the Western Front (1930) was banned in France until 1962
Blue Hawaii (1961), Elvis Presley's film, was banned in Malta because it showed women in bikinis
In the Realm of the Senses (1975) was banned in Britain until 1991 because of its explicit sexual content
Giant (1956) was banned in Syria because its star, Elizabeth Taylor, was deemed to be pro-Israeli
Limelight (1952), Charlie Chaplin's film, was banned in the USA for twenty years
Freaks (1932), the classic horror film, was banned in Britain for over thirty years
Let There be Light (1945), the John Huston film about shell-shocked American soldiers, was banned in the USA for nearly forty years
Hamlet (1948), Olivier's film version, was banned in China in 1964

The American Film Institute's ten greatest American movies of all time

Gone with the Wind (1939)
Citizen Kane (1941)
Casablanca (1942)
The African Queen (1952)
The Grapes of Wrath (1940)
One Flew Over the Cuckoo's Nest (1975)
Singin' in the Rain (1952)
Star Wars (1977)
2001: A Space Odyssey (1968)
The Wizard of Oz (1939)

Frankly, my dear, we do give a damn

Mel Gibson, Lethal Hamlet I

The ten most filmed stories
Cinderella
Hamlet
Carmen
Faust
Doctor Jekyll and Mr Hyde
Romeo and Juliet
Robinson Crusoe
La Dame aux Camélias
Don Quixote
The Three Musketeers

Ten movie stars who died in crashes
Françoise Dorléac: car, 1967
Leslie Howard: assumed plane, 1943
James Dean: car, 1955
Brandon de Wilde: car, 1972
Grace Kelly: car, 1982
Carole Lombard: plane, 1942
Will Rogers: plane, 1935
Tom Mix: car, 1940
Audie Murphy: plane, 1971
Jayne Mansfield: car, 1967

Ten left-handed movie stars
Rock Hudson
W.C. Fields
Marilyn Monroe
Charlie Chaplin
Judy Garland
Goldie Hawn
Robert Redford
Harpo Marx
Joanne Woodward
Betty Grable

Ten novelists who scripted movies
Martin Amis: *Saturn Three* (1980)
Fay Weldon: *The Life and Loves of a She Devil* (1989)
F. Scott Fitzgerald: *Three Comrades* (1938)
Raymond Chandler: *The Blue Dahlia* (1946)
Ernest Hemingway: *Spanish Earth* (1937)
William Faulkner: *The Road to Glory* (1936)
Beryl Bainbridge: *Sweet William* (1980)
Melvyn Bragg: *Isadora* (1968)
Edna O'Brien: *Zee and Co* (1971)
Arthur C. Clarke: *2001: A Space Odyssey* (1968)

Ten movie theme songs that went to Number One
'The Shoop-Shoop Song' by Cher: *Mermaids* (1991)
'A Groovy Kind of Love' by Phil Collins: *Buster* (1988)
'(Everything I Do) I Do It For You' by Bryan Adams: *Robin Hood: Prince of Thieves* (1991)
'Fame' by Irene Cara: *Fame* (1982)
'Take My Breath Away' by Berlin: *Top Gun* (1986)
'The One And Only' by Chesney Hawkes: *Buddy's Song* (1991)
'Stand By Me' by Ben E. King: *Stand By Me* (1987)
'Call Me' by Blondie: *American Gigolo* (1980)
'Night Fever' by The Bee Gees: *Saturday Night Fever* (1978)
'Unchained Melody' by The Righteous Brothers: *Ghost* (1990)

Ten movie stars with famous grandparents

Geraldine Chaplin: Eugene O'Neill
Daniel Day Lewis: Michael Balcon
Anjelica Huston: Walter Huston
Margaux Hemingway: Ernest Hemingway
Drew Barrymore: John Barrymore
Anne Baxter: Frank Lloyd Wright
Joely Richardson: Sir Michael Redgrave
Angela Lansbury: George Lansbury
Natasha Richardson: Sir Michael Redgrave
Mariel Hemingway: Ernest Hemingway

Ten actresses who tested for the part of Scarlett O'Hara

Lana Turner
Bette Davis
Loretta Young
Norma Shearer
Joan Crawford
Jean Harlow
Carole Lombard
Claudette Colbert
Katharine Hepburn
Ann Sheridan

Ten actresses who were beauty queens

Sylvia Kristel: Miss Television Europe, 1973
Cybill Shepherd: Miss Teenage Memphis, 1966
Michelle Pfeiffer: Miss Orange County, 1976
Kim Novak: Miss Deepfreeze, 1953
Raquel Welch: Miss Photogenic, 1953
Dyan Cannon: Miss West Seattle, 1957
Sophia Loren: Miss Elegance, 1950
Claudia Cardinale: The Most Beautiful Italian Girl in Tunis, 1956
Lauren Bacall: Miss Greenwich Village, 1942
Debbie Reynolds: Miss Burbank, 1948

Bette Davis – tomorrow is another role

Sophia, so good

Ten pairs of movie stars born on the same day

Glenda Jackson and Albert Finney: 9 May 1936
George Peppard and Laurence Harvey: 1 October 1928
Meryl Streep and Lindsay Wagner: 22 June 1949
Marlon Brandon and Doris Day: 3 April 1924
Diana Rigg and Natalie Wood: 20 July 1938
Karen Black and Genevieve Bujold: 1 July 1942
Lee J. Cobb and Broderick Crawford: 9 December 1911
Alan Bates and Barry Humphries: 17 February 1934
Diahann Carroll and Donald Sutherland: 17 July 1935
Stephen Boyd and Gina Lollobrigida: 4 July 1928

Ten famous people born on the same day as a movie star

Pik Botha and Anouk Aimée: 24 April 1932
The Bishop of Durham and Paul Newman: 26 January 1925
Willie Rushton and Robert Redford: 18 August 1937
Charlie Watts and Stacy Keach: 2 June 1941
Tony Blackburn and Katharine Ross: 29 January 1943
Dickie Bird and Jayne Mansfield: 19 April 1933
Paul Heiney and Jessica Lange: 20 April 1949
Boris Spassky and Vanessa Redgrave: 30 January 1937
Ian Dury and Susan Hampshire: 12 May 1942
Quincy Jones and Michael Caine: 14 March 1933

Ten people who took their mother's surname

Marilyn Monroe: father's name Mortenson
Leslie Howard: father's name Stainer
Rita Hayworth: father's name Cansino
Patti Davis: daughter of Nancy Davis and Ronald Reagan
Simone Signoret: father's name Kaminker
Gloria Grahame: father's name Hallward
Shelley Winters: father's name Schrift
Shirley Maclaine: father's name Beaty
Jean Harlow: father's name Carpentier
Mario Lanza: father's name Cocozza

Hot properties – ten items of movie memorabilia sold at auction

Charlie Chaplin's hat and cane: £82,500 (Christie's, 1987)
Charlie Chaplin's boots: £38,500 (Christie's, 1987)
Marilyn Monroe's black satin dress from *Some Like It Hot*: £19,800 (Christie's, 1988)
Model of Boris Karloff as Frankenstein's monster: £16,500 (Christie's, 1988)
Giant boots worn by Elton John in *Tommy*: £12,100 (Sotheby's, 1988)
Laurel and Hardy's hats: £11,000 (Christie's, 1989)
Cape worn by Prince in *Purple Rain*: £7,150 (Sotheby's, 1990)
Marilyn Monroe's black stiletto shoes from *Some Like It Hot*: £5,500 (Sotheby's, 1989)
Promotional thermometer for *Some Like It Hot* featuring Marilyn Monroe down the centre: £5,060 (Phillips, 1989)
A pair of black suede stiletto shoes worn by Marilyn Monroe in *Let's Make Love*: £3,520 (Phillips, 1990)

The ten most successful Bond themes

'A View to a Kill': Duran Duran (reached No. 2 in the charts) *A View to a Kill* (1985)
'The Living Daylights': A-Ha (reached No. 5 in the charts) *The Living Daylights* (1987)
'Licence To Kill': Gladys Knight (reached No. 6 in the charts) *Licence to Kill* (1989)
'Nobody Does It Better': Carly Simon (reached No. 7 in the charts) *The Spy Who Loved Me* (1977)
'For Your Eyes Only': Sheena Easton (reached No. 8 in the charts) *For Your Eyes Only* (1981)
'Live and Let Die': Wings (reached No. 9 in the charts) *Live and Let Die* (1973)
'You Only Live Twice': Nancy Sinatra (reached No. 11 in the charts) *You Only Live Twice* (1967)
'James Bond Theme': John Barry (reached No. 13 in the charts) *Dr No* (1962)
'From Russia with Love': Matt Monro (reached No. 20 in the charts) *From Russia With Love* (1963)
'Goldfinger': Shirley Bassey (reached No. 21 in the charts) *Goldfinger* (1964)

Boris – what a Pratt

James Dean, rebel without a pension

Ten movie stars who wisely changed their names

Sandra Dee: Alexandra Zuck
Boris Karloff: William Pratt
Cyd Charisse: Tula Finklea
Mel Brooks: Melvin Kaminsky
Lois Maxwell: Lois Hooker
Red Buttons: Aaron Chwatt
Diana Dors: Diana Fluck
Roy Rogers: Leonard Slye
Jane Wyman: Sarah Jane Fulks
Albert Brooks: Albert Einstein

Gone, but not forgotten – ten stars and the ages they would've reached this year

Marilyn Monroe, 66
Montgomery Clift, 72
Jean Seberg, 54
John Cazale, 56
Steve McQueen, 62
Jean Harlow, 81
James Dean, 61
Natalie Wood, 54
Elvis Presley, 57
Peter Sellers, 67

Ten movie stars known by their middle names

Patrick *Ryan* O'Neal
Terence *Steve* McQueen
Charles *Robert* Redford
Eldred *Gregory* Peck
James *David* Niven
William *Clark* Gable
Robert *Oliver* Reed
Michael *Sylvester* Stallone
Henry *Warren* Beatty
John *Anthony* Quinn

Ten Hollywood stars who were born in Britain

Ray Milland
Madeleine Carroll
Boris Karloff
Charlie Chaplin
Stan Laurel
Bob Hope
Victor McLaglen
Roddy McDowall
Ronald Colman
Cary Grant

Ten actors who committed suicide

Carole Landis, apparently upset over a relationship with Rex Harrison, took an overdose in the bath (1948)

Helen Twelvetrees, a stalwart of melodramas and soap-operas, took an overdose (1958)

Phyllis Haver, the former Mack Sennet bathing beauty who became a leading lady in Hollywood, took an overdose of barbiturates (1960)

Margaret Sullivan, whose husbands included Henry Fonda and William Wyler, died of an overdose of barbiturates (1960)

Clara Blandick, Aunt Em in *The Wizard of Oz*, suffocated herself with a plastic bag (1962)

George Reeves, Superman in the TV series, shot himself in Hollywood (1959)

Jonathan Hale, Mr Dithers in the *Blondie* series, shot himself (1966)

Albert Dekker, who played the title role in *Dr Cyclops*, hung himself (1968)

George Sanders took an overdose of sleeping tablets, citing boredom as the main reason (1972)

Gig Young shot his bride of three weeks before turning the gun on himself (1978)

Hope on the road from Blighty

Laurel – born in Britain, made in Hollywood

Ten brainy actors

Telly Savalas: MA in psychology, Columbia
    University
Kathleen Turner: BA in fine art and theatre,
    University of Maryland
Richard Chamberlain: BA in art, Pomona
    College, California
William Hurt: BA in theology, Tufts University
Paul Newman: BA in English, Keynon College,
    Ohio
Kevin Kline: BA in drama, Indiana University
Sam Waterstone: BA in French and History, Yale
    University
William Shatner: BA in law, McGill University
Jack Lemmon: BA in drama, Harvard
Charles Boyer: Degree in philosophy, Sorbonne

Dyb, dyb, dyb: ten actors who were Boy Scouts

Bernard Bresslaw
Gordon Jackson
Roy Kinnear
Roger Rees
Derek Nimmo
Richard Attenborough
Norman Wisdom
James Stewart
Brian Rix
Lionel Jeffries

'My dad was . . . ' Ten stars' fathers' jobs

Harrison Ford: milkman
Albert Finney: bookmaker
Faye Dunaway: sergeant in US Army
Roger Moore: policeman
Candice Bergen: ventriloquist
Daniel Day Lewis: poet laureate
Burt Reynolds: police chief
Ben Kingsley: doctor
Jean-Paul Belmondo: sculptor
Kris Kristofferson: US Air Force general

What's a BA, Michael? Er . . . Kathleen Turner and
Michael Douglas in *Jewel of the Nile*

How ten movie stars were discovered

Gina Lollobrigida was studying to become a
    commercial artist when movie director Mario
    Costa approached her in a street in Rome. After
    La Lolla had finished haranguing him for
    accosting her, Costa asked her to test for his
    next movie.
George Raft, a small-time racketeer, was sent to
    put pressure on a nightclub owner, Texas
    Guinan, and was offered a part in her movie
    Queen of the Nightclubs as a pay-off
Fatty Arbuckle, a plumber's mate, was signed up
    by Mack Sennett the day Arbuckle came round
    to unblock the producer's drain
Lana Turner was just fifteen when a talent scout
    spotted her sipping soda in an ice-cream parlour
    in Hollywood
Walter Brennan got his first break when he
    stepped in and offered to do the voice-over for a
    stubborn donkey who refused to bray on a
    movie set
Ryan O'Neal was discovered working out in a gym
    by actor Richard Egan
Valerie Perrine's break came when she
    encountered a Hollywood agent at a roommate's
    birthday party
John Wayne was plucked out of the props
    department at the Fox Studios in Hollywood
At fifteen Ida Lupino was selected to play a
    precocious teenager after her own mother, the
    actress Connie Emerald, auditioned for the part
    but was considered too old
When Johnny Weissmuller arrived at a film studio
    to visit his friend Clark Gable, he found the only
    way to slip through the gates was to join a group
    of young actors auditioning for the role of
    Tarzan. To his astonishment, Weissmuller got
    the part

Ten playwrights who married actresses

Robert Bolt: Sarah Miles
Jack Rosenthal: Maureen Lipman
Garson Kanin: Ruth Gordon
Arthur Miller: Marilyn Monroe
Neil Simon: Marsha Mason
Harold Pinter: Vivien Merchant
Kurt Weill: Lotte Lenya
Mike Leigh: Alison Steadman
Sam Shepard: Jessica Lange
John Osborne: Jill Bennett

Ten books chosen by movie stars on *Desert Island Discs*

Dirk Bogarde: *Akenfield* by Ronald Blythe
Gloria Swanson: *The Prophet* by Kahlil Gibran
Stewart Granger: The collected works of Ernest
    Hemingway
Jack Lemmon: *At Play in the Fields of the Lord* by
    Peter Matthiessen
Roger Moore: *Noble House* by James Clavell
John Gielgud: *A La Recherche du Temps Perdu* by
    Marcel Proust
Natalie Wood: The poetry of e.e. cummings
Gregory Peck: *Abraham Lincoln* by Carl
    Sandburg
Joan Collins: The complete works of Oscar Wilde
Helen Mirren: The Bhagavad-Gita

Bruce Willis, Germany's leading *Liebling*?

And I'm leaving the electric page-turner at home –
Roger Moore

Ten stars born in unlikely places

Bruce Willis: West Germany
Victoria Principal: Japan
Stephanie Beacham: Morocco
Julie Christie: India
Audrey Hepburn: Belgium
Olivia Hussey: Argentina
Edward G. Robinson: Romania
Harry H. Corbett: Burma
Fiona Fullerton: Nigeria
Nicola Pagett: Egypt

Ten actors who were teachers

Madeleine Carroll
Michael Redgrave
Agnes Moorehead
Windsor Davies
Patricia Hodge
George C. Scott
Madeline Kahn
Michael Hordern
Brian Glover
Monty Woolley

Ronald checked in . . .

. . . Michelle checked out

Ten actresses' former jobs

Michelle Pfeiffer: supermarket assistant
Greta Garbo: barber's assistant
Julie Walters: nurse
Madonna: waitress
Valerie Perrine: stripper
Glenda Jackson: sales assistant in Boots
Diana Rigg: coffee-bar assistant
Lauren Bacall: cover girl
Barbara Stanwyck: shop assistant
Raquel Welch: waitress

Ten actors' former jobs

Jeremy Irons: social worker
Charlton Heston: artists' model
Burt Lancaster: circus acrobat
Sean Connery: French polisher
Ronald Reagan: lifeguard
Gregory Peck: tour guide
Alan Alda: taxi driver
Danny de Vito: hairdresser
Charles Bronson: miner
Burt Reynolds: American footballer

Ten actors who appeared in *Coronation Street*

Joanna Lumley
Mollie Sugden
Ben Kingsley
Prunella Scales
Davy Jones
Richard Beckinsale
Max Wall
Martin Shaw
Arthur Lowe
Michael Elphick

Worth the price of a ticket? Ten of the longest films of all time

The Cure for Insomnia (1987): 85 hours
Mondo Teeth (1970): 50 hours
The Longest Most Meaningless Movie in the World (1970): 48 hours
The Burning of the Red Lotus Temple (1928–31): 27 hours
The Journey (1987): 14 hours, 33 minutes
The Old Testament (1922): 13 hours
Comment Yukong Déplace les Montagnes (How Yukong Moved the Mountains) (1976): 12 hours, 43 minutes
Nigen No Joken (The Human Condition) (1958–60): 9 hours, 29 minutes
Voina I Mir (War & Peace) (1963–67): 8 hours, 27 minutes
Foolish Wives (1922): 6 hours, 24 minutes

Ten American movies that have won the Best Film Award from the British Film Academy

The Graduate (1969)
Midnight Cowboy (1970)
Butch Cassidy and the Sundance Kid (1971)
Cabaret (1973)
Alice Doesn't Live Here Any More (1976)
One Flew Over the Cuckoo's Nest (1977)
Annie Hall (1978)
Julia (1979)
Manhattan (1980)
The Purple Rose of Cairo (1986)

Ten movies that have won the Palme d'Or at the Cannes Film Festival

The Knack (1965)
Blow-Up (1967)
If (1969)
M*A*S*H (1970)
The Go-Between (1971)
The Conversation (1974)
Taxi Driver (1976)
Paris, Texas (1984)
The Mission (1986)
sex, lies and videotape (1989)

The ten top box-office draws of the past decade (male)

Burt Reynolds (1982)
Clint Eastwood (1983)
Clint Eastwood (1984)
Sylvester Stallone (1985)
Tom Cruise (1986)
Eddie Murphy (1987)
Tom Cruise (1988)
Jack Nicholson (1989)
Arnold Schwarzenegger (1990)
Kevin Costner (1991)

The ten top box-office draws of the past decade (female)

Dolly Parton (1982)
Meryl Streep (1983)
Sally Field (1984)
Meryl Streep (1985)
Bette Midler (1986)
Glenn Close (1987)
Bette Midler (1988)
Kathleen Turner (1989)
Julia Roberts (1990)
Julia Roberts (1991)

Tom shakes it up . . .

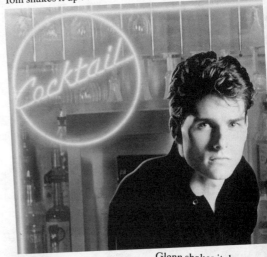

. . . Glenn shakes it down . . .

. . . and Dolly shakes it about

OSCARS

Ten things that happen at every Oscar ceremony

Cher's outfit will reveal even more than it did the
    previous year
Woody Allen won't turn up
Someone very old indeed will shuffle on to a
    standing ovation
Steven Spielberg won't win anything
Someone will make an embarrassing political
    speech
Nobody will have heard of the best foreign
    language film
Every winner will thank at least three people
Every loser will smile and clap vigorously when the
    winners are announced
Britain will be able to claim some link with the
    special effects award
There'll be a special tribute to someone whose
    films appear only on BBC2 on Saturday
    afternoons

The first ten movies to win the Best Film Oscar

Wings (1928)
Broadway Melody (1929)
All Quiet on the Western Front (1930)
Cimarron (1931)
Grand Hotel (1932)
Cavalcade (1933)
It Happened One Night (1934)
Mutiny on the Bounty (1935)
The Great Ziegfeld (1936)
The Life of Emile Zola (1937)

And I'd like to thank my dress designer, if I had one –
Cher

Classic movies that didn't win a single Oscar

A Star is Born (Judy Garland version, 1954)
The Maltese Falcon (1941)
High Society (1956)
The Caine Mutiny (1954)
Twelve Angry Men (1957)
Rebel Without a Cause (1955)
Psycho (1960)
Double Indemnity (1944)
Brief Encounter (1945)
Singin' in the Rain (1952)

The first ten winners of the Best Actress Oscar

Janet Gaynor: *Seventh Heaven* (1928)
Mary Pickford: *Coquette* (1929)
Norma Shearer: *The Divorcee* (1930)
Marie Dressler: *Min and Bill* (1931)
Helen Hayes: *Sin of Madelon Claudet* (1932)
Katharine Hepburn: *Morning Glory* (1933)
Claudette Colbert: *It Happened One Night* (1934)
Bette Davis: *Dangerous* (1935)
Luise Rainer: *The Great Ziegfeld* (1936)
Luise Rainer: *The Good Earth* (1937)

Katharine Hepburn, all set for Oscar glory

The first ten winners of the Best Actor Oscar

Emil Jannings: *The Last Command* (1928)
Warner Baxter: *In Old Arizona* (1929)
George Arliss: *Disraeli* (1930)
Lionel Barrymore: *A Free Soul* (1931)
Frederic March: *Dr Jekyll and Mr Hyde* and
    Wallace Beery: *The Champ* (1932)
Charles Laughton: *The Private Life of Henry VIII* (1933)
Clark Gable: *It Happened One Night* (1934)
Victor McLaglen: *The Informer* (1935)
Paul Muni: *The Story of Louis Pasteur* (1936)
Spencer Tracy: *Captains Courageous* (1937)

Ten beastly Oscar winners

The Lion in Winter (1968): best actress, Katharine
    Hepburn
The Deer Hunter (1978): best film
Raging Bull (1980): best actor, Robert De Niro
Save the Tiger (1973): best actor, Jack Lemmon
Who Framed Roger Rabbit (1988): best visual
    effects
Cat Ballou (1965): best actor, Lee Marvin
To Kill a Mockingbird (1962): best actor, Gregory
    Peck
One Flew Over the Cuckoo's Nest (1975): best film
The Kiss of the Spider Woman (1985): best actor,
    William Hurt
A Fish Called Wanda (1988): best supporting
    actor, Kevin Kline

Ten actors who've gone on to win non-acting Oscars

Warren Beatty: director, *Reds* (1981)
Keith Carradine: best original song, 'I'm Easy', for
    Nashville (1975)
Laurence Olivier: director, for *Hamlet* (1948)
Colin Welland: writer, for *Chariots of Fire* (1981)
Kevin Costner: director, for *Dances with Wolves*
    (1991)
Charlie Chaplin: best original dramatic score, for
    Limelight (1972)
Orson Welles: writer, for *Citizen Kane* (1941)
Michael Douglas: producer, for *One Flew Over the
    Cuckoo's Nest* (1975)
Robert Redford: director, for *Ordinary People*
    (1980)
Richard Attenborough: director, for *Gandhi
    (1982)*

Robinson, never a G man

Rogers and Astaire – an honorary affair

Oscar wild – ten Brits who won the Best Actor Academy Award

Charles Laughton: *The Private Life of Henry VIII* (1933)
Robert Donat: *Goodbye, Mr Chips* (1939)
Laurence Olivier: *Hamlet* (1948)
Alec Guinness: *Bridge on the River Kwai* (1957)
David Niven: *Separate Tables* (1958)
Rex Harrison: *My Fair Lady* (1964)
Paul Scofield: *A Man for all Seasons* (1966)
Ben Kingsley: *Gandhi* (1982)
Daniel Day Lewis: *My Left Foot* (1990)
Jeremy Irons: *Reversal of Fortune* (1991)

Ten actors who won only honorary Oscars

Fred Astaire
Edward G. Robinson
Judy Garland
Bob Hope
Gene Kelly
Greta Garbo
Groucho Marx
Shirley Temple
Cary Grant
Danny Kaye

Ten people who've won three or more Oscars

Walt Disney: 32
Edith Head: 8
John Ford: 4
Katharine Hepburn: 4
Frank Capra: 3
William Wyler: 3
Walter Brennan: 3
Ingrid Bergman: 3
Billy Wilder: 6
Francis Coppola: 5

Burton – always a loser

Always the bridesmaid never the bride – Oscar nominees who never won the glittering prize

Richard Burton (seven nominations)
Peter O'Toole (seven nominations)
Deborah Kerr (six nominations)
Alfred Hitchcock (five nominations)
Arthur Kennedy (five nominations)
Al Pacino (five nominations)
Mickey Rooney (four nominations)
Albert Finney (four nominations)
Marsha Mason (four nominations)
Glenn Close (four nominations)

Ten surprising Oscar nominees

John Travolta (*Saturday Night Fever*), 1978
Rock Hudson (*Giant*), 1956
Telly Savalas (*The Birdman of Alcatraz*), 1961
Mikhail Baryshnikov (*The Turning Point*), 1977
Sylvester Stallone (*Rocky*), 1976
Bobby Darin (*Captain Newman, MD*), 1963
Peter Falk (*Murder, Inc.*), 1960
Oprah Winfrey (*The Color Purple*), 1985
Jack Wild (*Oliver!*), 1968
Jack Palance (*Sudden Fear*), 1952

A 1–10 of Oscar-winning films

Klute (1971): one Oscar
Aliens (1986): two
A Room with a View (1985): three
Platoon (1986): four
Who's Afraid of Virginia Woolf? (1966): five
The Godfather Part II (1974): six
Out of Africa (1985): seven
Gandhi (1982): eight
The Last Emperor (1987): nine
West Side Story (1961): ten

Ten actresses who've won two Oscars

(BA = best actress, BS = best supporting actress)
Bette Davis: *Dangerous* (1935) BA; *Jezebel* (1938) BA
Olivia de Havilland: *To Each His Own* (1946) BA; *The Heiress* (1949) BA
Shelley Winters: *The Diary of Anne Frank* (1959) BS; *A Patch of Blue* (1965) BS
Meryl Streep: *Kramer versus Kramer* (1979) BS; *Sophie's Choice* (1982) BA
Vivien Leigh: *Gone with the Wind* (1939) BA; *A Streetcar Named Desire* (1951) BA
Sally Field: *Norma Rae* (1979) BA; *Places in the Heart* (1984) BA
Glenda Jackson: *Women in Love* (1970) BA; *A Touch of Class* (1973) BA
Elizabeth Taylor: *Butterfield 8* (1960) BA; *Who's Afraid of Virginia Woolf?* (1966) BA
Jane Fonda: *Klute* (1971) BA; *Coming Home* (1978) BA
Maggie Smith: *The Prime of Miss Jean Brodie* (1969) BA; *California Suite* (1978) BS

Taylor – two times a winner

Spencer went bananas, twice

Ten actors who've won two Oscars

(BA = best actor, BS = best supporting actor)

Marlon Brando: *On the Waterfront* (1954) BA; *The Godfather* (1972) BA (refused)

Peter Ustinov: *Spartacus* (1960) BS; *Topkapi* (1964) BS

Fredric March: *Dr Jekyll and Mr Hyde* (1932) BA; *Best Years of Our Lives* (1946) BA

Jack Nicholson: *One Flew Over the Cuckoo's Nest* (1975) BA; *Terms of Endearment* (1983) BS

Gary Cooper: *Sergeant York* (1941) BA; *High Noon* (1952) BA

Jack Lemmon: *Mister Roberts* (1955) BS; *Save the Tiger* (1973) BA

Dustin Hoffman: *Kramer versus Kramer* (1979) BA; *Rain Man* (1989) BA

Spencer Tracy: *Captains Courageous* (1937) BA; *Boys' Town* (1938) BA

Anthony Quinn: *Viva Zapata!* (1952) BS; *Lust for Life* (1956) BS

Robert de Niro: *The Godfather Part II* (1974) BS; *Raging Bull* (1980) BA

Ten Oscar-winning songs

'White Christmas' (*Holiday Inn*), 1942

'Moon River' (*Breakfast at Tiffany's*), 1961

'Buttons and Bows' (*The Paleface*), 1948

'Raindrops Keep Falling On My Head' (*Butch Cassidy and the Sundance Kid*), 1969

'Fame' (*Fame*), 1980

'Over the Rainbow' (*The Wizard of Oz*), 1939

'Zip-A-Dee-Doo-Dah' (*Song of the South*), 1946

'High Hopes' (*A Hole in the Head*), 1959

'The Windmills of Your Mind' (*The Thomas Crown Affair*), 1968

'Chim Chim Cher-ee' (*Mary Poppins*), 1964

Ten songs that were nominated but didn't win Oscars

'Cheek to Cheek': *Top Hat* (1935)

'Alfie': *Alfie* (1966)

'Chatanooga Choo-Choo': *Sun Valley Serenade* (1941)

'Unchained Melody': *Unchained* (1955)

'That Old Black Magic': *Star Spangled Rhythm* (1943)

'The Look of Love': *Casino Royale* (1967)

'I've Got You Under My Skin': *Born to Dance* (1936)

'The Trolley Song': *Meet Me in St Louis* (1944)

'Ben': *Ben* (1972)

'I've Got a Girl in Kalamazoo': *Orchestra Wives* (1942)

Ten forgotten movies that were nominated for the Best Film Oscar

The Snake Pit (1948)

The Sounder (1972)

A Soldier's Story (1984)

America, America (1963)

Crossfire (1947)

Battleground (1949)

The Emigrants (1972)

The Russians are Coming, The Russians are Coming (1966)

Decision Before Dawn (1951)

Fanny (1961)

NOW STARRING...

Ten actors who've played themselves in movies

Humphrey Bogart: *The Love Lottery* (1953)
Michael York: *Fedora* (1978)
Orson Welles: *Follow the Boys* (1944)
Charlie Chaplin: *Show People* (1929)
Frank Sinatra: *Cannonball Run II* (1983)
Larry Hagman: *I Am Blushing* (1981)
Bing Crosby: *Let's Make Love* (1960)
Martin Sheen: *The King of Prussia* (1982)
Sid James: *The Beauty Contest* (1964)
Ronald Reagan: *It's a Great Feeling* (1949)

Ten actresses who've played themselves in movies

Anne Bancroft: *Silent Movie* (1976)
Bette Davis: *Hollywood Canteen* (1944)
Julie Christie: *Nashville* (1975)
Gloria Swanson: *Airport* (1974)
Katharine Hepburn: *Stage Door Canteen* (1943)
Dorothy Lamour: *Duffy's Tavern* (1945)
Liv Ullman: *Players* (1979)
Natalie Wood: *Willie and Phil* (1981)
Susannah York: *Long Shot* (1978)
Liza Minnelli: *The Muppets Take Manhattan* (1984)

Ten actors who've played the devil

Jack Nicholson: *The Witches of Eastwick* (1987)
Ernest Borgnine: *The Devil's Rain* (1975)
Peter Cook: *Bedazzled* (1967)
Juliet Mills: *The Devil Within Her* (1974)
Vincent Price: *The Story of Mankind* (1957)
Burgess Meredith: *The Sentinel* (1976)
Linda Blair: *The Exorcist* (1973)
Ray Milland: *Alias Nick Beal* (1949)
Yves Montand: *Marguerite of the Night* (1955)
Robert De Niro: *Angel Heart* (1987)

Ten movie stars who've been played by movie stars

Joan Crawford: by Faye Dunaway in *Mommie Dearest* (1981)
W.C. Fields: by Rod Steiger in *W.C. Fields and Me* (1976)
Buster Keaton: by Donald O'Connor in *The Buster Keaton Story* (1957)
Jean Harlow: by Carroll Baker in *Harlow* (1965)
Frances Farmer: by Jessica Lange in *Frances* (1982)
Carole Lombard: by Jill Clayburgh in *Gable and Lombard* (1976)
Rudolph Valentino: by Franco Nero in *The Legend of Valentino* (1975)
Lon Chaney Sr: by James Cagney in *Man of a Thousand Faces* (1957)
John Barrymore: by Errol Flynn in *Too Much Too Soon* (1958)
Bruce Lee: by Bruce Li in *Bruce Lee – the True Story* :1976)

Ten actors who've played Frankenstein's monster

Boris Karloff: *Frankenstein* (1931)
Elsa Lanchester: *Bride of Frankenstein* (1935)
Lon Chaney Jr: *The Ghost of Frankenstein* (1942)
Bela Lugosi: *Frankenstein Meets the Wolf Man* (1943)
Glenn Strange: *Abbott and Costello Meet Frankenstein* (1948)
Christopher Lee: *The Curse of Frankenstein* (1957)
Gary Conway: *I Was A Teenage Frankenstein* (1957)
Freddie Jones: *Frankenstein Must Be Destroyed* (1969)
Dave Prowse: *Frankenstein and the Monster From Hell* (1973)
Michael Sarrazin: *Frankenstein: The True Story* (1974)

Darling, I'm bewitched – James Stewart and Kim Novak in *Bell, Book and Candle*

Ten actresses who've played witches

Margaret Hamilton: *The Wizard of Oz* (1939)
Veronica Lake: *I Married a Witch* (1942)
Kim Novak: *Bell, Book and Candle* (1958)
Ruth Gordon: *Rosemary's Baby* (1968)
Lana Turner: *Witches' Brew* (1980)
Faye Dunaway: *Supergirl* (1984)
Michelle Pfeiffer: *The Witches of Eastwick* (1987)
Bette Davis: *Wicked Stepmother* (1988)
Anjelica Huston: *The Witches* (1990)
Geraldine McEwan: *Robin Hood: Prince of Thieves* (1991)

Ten actors who've played Hitler

Charlie Chaplin: *The Great Dictator* (1940)
Anthony Hopkins: *The Bunker* (1981)
Richard Basehart: *Hitler* (1961)
Ludwig Donath: *The Strange Death of Adolf Hitler* (1943)
Derek Jacobi: *Inside The Third Reich* (1982)
Dick Shawn: *The Producers* (1967)
Luther Adler: *The Desert Fox* (1951)
Alec Guiness: *Hitler: The Last Ten Days* (1973)
Robert Watson: *The Hitler Gang* (1944)
Kenneth Griffith: *The Two-Headed Spy* (1958)

Ten actresses who've played hookers (happy or otherwise)

Shirley Maclaine: *Irma la Douce* (1963)
Sophia Loren: *Lady L* (1965)
Carroll Baker: *Sylvia* (1964)
Nancy Kwan: *The World of Suzie Wong* (1960)
Melina Mercouri: *Never on Sunday* (1959)
Jane Fonda: *Klute* (1971)
Julia Roberts: *Pretty Woman* (1990)
Catherine Deneuve: *Belle de Jour* (1967)
Diane Cilento: *Rattle of a Simple Man* (1964)
Carol White: *Poor Cow* (1967)

Ten actresses who've played Cleopatra

Hildegard Neil: *Antony and Cleopatra* (1972)
Linda Cristal: *Legions of the Nile* (1959)
Claudette Colbert: *Cleopatra* (1934)
Sophia Loren: *Due Notti con Cleopatra* (1954)
Vivien Leigh: *Caesar and Cleopatra* (1946)
Rhonda Fleming: *Serpent of the Nile* (1953)
Elizabeth Taylor: *Cleopatra* (1963)
Amanda Barrie: *Carry on Cleo* (1965)
Hedy Lamarr: *The Story of Mankind* (1957)
Theda Bara: *Cleopatra* (1917)

The Marlowe Syndrome – ten actors who've walked down those mean Chandler streets

Lloyd Nolan in *Time to Kill* (1942) based on *The High Window*

Michael Arlen in *The Falcon Takes Over* (1942) based on *Farewell, My Lovely*

Dick Powell in *Murder, My Sweet* (1944) based on *Farewell, My Lovely*

Robert Montgomery in *The Lady in the Lake* (1946) based on *The Lady in the Lake*

Humphrey Bogart in *The Big Sleep* (1946) based on *The Big Sleep*

George Montgomery in *The Brasher Doubloon* (1947) based on *The High Window*

James Garner in *Marlowe* (1969) based on *The Little Sister*

Elliot Gould in *The Long Goodbye* (1973) based on *The Long Goodbye*

Robert Mitchum in *Farewell, My Lovely* (1975) based on *Farewell, My Lovely*

Robert Mitchum (again!) in *The Big Sleep* (1978) based on *The Big Sleep*

Ten actors who've played more than one role in the same film

Sean Young: *A Kiss Before Dying* (1991) 2 parts

Mark Lester: *The Prince and the Pauper* (1977) 2 parts

Alec Guinness: *Kind Hearts And Coronets* (1949) 8 parts

Elvis Presley: *Kissin' Cousins* (1963) 2 parts

Peter Sellers: *Dr Strangelove* (1963) 3 parts

Lionel Jeffries: *The Secret of My Success* (1965) 4 parts

Rod Steiger: *No Way to Treat a Lady* (1968) 7 parts

Deborah Kerr: *The Life and Death of Colonel Blimp* (1943) 3 parts

Jerry Lewis: *The Nutty Professor* (1963) 2 parts

Charlie Chaplin: *The Great Dictator* (1940) 2 parts

Ten people who co-starred with Elvis Presley

Walter Matthau: *King Creole* (1958)

Angela Lansbury: *Blue Hawaii* (1961)

Charles Bronson: *Kid Galahad* (1962)

Ursula Andress: *Fun in Acapulco* (1963)

Burgess Meredith: *Stay Away Joe* (1968)

Ann-Margret: *Viva Las Vegas* (1964)

Vincent Price: *The Trouble With Girls* (1969)

Barbara Stanwyck: *Roustabout* (1964)

Mary Tyler Moore: *Change of Habit* (1969)

Elsa Lanchester: *Easy Come, Easy Go* (1966)

Robert Mitchum – double trouble

We are quite amused – ten actresses who've played Queen Victoria

Fay Compton: *The Prime Minister* (1941)

Anna Neagle: *Sixty Glorious Years* (1938)

Muriel Aked: *The Story of Gilbert and Sullivan* (1953)

Romy Schneider: *The Young Victoria* (1955)

Irene Dunne: *The Mudlark* (1950)

Susan Field: *The Adventures of Sherlock Holmes' Smarter Brother* (1975)

Helena Pickard: *The Lady with the Lamp* (1951)

Sybil Thorndike: *Melba* (1953)

Mollie Maureen: *The Private Life of Sherlock Holmes* (1970)

Margaret Mann: *Disraeli* (1929)

Two beautiful lassies – Liz Taylor and faithful friend

Ten actresses who've played Queen Elizabeth I

Bette Davis: *The Private Lives of Elizabeth and Essex* (1939)
Glenda Jackson: *Mary, Queen of Scots* (1972)
Sarah Bernhardt: *Queen Elizabeth* (1912)
Dame Flora Robson: *The Sea Hawk* (1940)
Athene Seyler: *Drake of England* (1935)
Jean Simmons: *Young Bess* (1953)
Lalla Ward: *The Prince and the Pauper* (1977)
Agnes Moorehead: *The Story of Mankind* (1957)
Jenny Runacre: *Jubilee* (1978)
Irene Worth: *Seven Seas to Calais* (1963)

Ten actors who've played US presidents

Frank Windsor: George Washington (*Revolution*, 1986)
Henry Fonda: Abraham Lincoln (*Young Mr Lincoln*, 1939)
Alexander Knox: Woodrow Wilson (*Wilson*, 1944)
Ralph Bellamy: Franklin D Roosevelt (*Sunrise at Campobello*, 1960)
James Whitmore: Harry Truman (*Give 'Em Hell, Harry!*, 1975)
Cliff Robertson: John F Kennedy (*PT 109*, 1963)
Charlton Heston: Andrew Jackson (*The President's Lady*, 1953)
Jason Robards: Ulysses Grant (*The Legend of the Lone Ranger*, 1981)
Brian Keith: Theodore Roosevelt (*The Wind and the Lion*, 1975)
Burgess Meredith: James Madison (*The Magnificent Doll*, 1946)

It's a dog's life – ten cinematic canines

Hooch: *Turner and Hooch* (1989)
Lassie: *Lassie Come Home* (1943)
Toto: *The Wizard of Oz* (1939)
Rin Tin Tin: *Jaws of Steel* (1927)
Asta: *The Thin Man* (1934)
Daisy: *Blondie* (1938)
Digby: *Digby: The Biggest Dog in the World* (1973)
Won Ton Ton: *Won Ton Ton, the Dog Who Saved Hollywood* (1976)
Bullseye: *Oliver Twist* (1948)
Greyfriars Bobby: *Greyfriars Bobby* (1960)

Ten actors who've played Dracula

Lon Chaney Jr: *Son of Dracula* (1943)
David Niven: *Vampire* (1975)
Dennis Price: *Vampyros Lesbos* (1970)
John Carradine: *Nocturna* (1979)
Christopher Lee: *Dracula, Pere et Fils* (1976)
George Hamilton: *Love at First Bite* (1979)
Bela Lugosi: *Dracula* (1931)
Francis Lederer: *The Return of Dracula* (1958)
Klaus Kinski: *Nosferatu, the Vampyre* (1979)
Frank Langella: *Dracula* (1979)

Sean Connery, a hunk of a monk

Again, Josephine? Ten actors who've played Napoleon

Charles Boyer: *Maria Walewska* (1937)
Marlon Brando: *Desirée* (1954)
Kenneth Haigh: *Eagle in a Cage* (1971)
Ian Holm: *Time Bandits* (1981)
Claude Rains: *Hearts Divided* (1936)
Herbert Lom: *The Young Mr Pitt* (1942)
Rod Steiger: *Waterloo* (1971)
Dennis Hopper: *The Story of Mankind* (1957)
Paul Muni: *Seven Faces* (1929)
Eli Wallach: *The Adventures of Gerard* (1970)

Ten actors who've played Billy the Kid

Audie Murphy: *Texas Kid Outlaw* (1950)
Paul Newman: *The Left-Handed Gun* (1958)
Jean-Pierre Leaud: *A Girl is a Gun* (1971)
Kris Kristofferson: *Pat Garrett and Billy The Kid* (1973)
Johnny Mack Brown: *Billy the Kid* (1930)
Buster Crabbe: *Raiders of Red Rock* (1946)
Robert Taylor: *Billy the Kid* (1941)
Val Kilmer: *Billy the Kid* (1988)
Roy Rogers: *Billy the Kid Returns* (1938)
Michael J. Pollard: *Dirty Little Billy* (1972)

Ten actors who've got into the habit (religious, that is)

Sean Connery: *The Name of the Rose* (1986)
Joan Collins: *Sea Wife* (1957)
Mike McShane: *Robin Hood: Prince of Thieves* (1991)
Anne Bancroft: *Agnes of God* (1985)
Pat O'Brien: *Angels with Dirty Faces* (1938)
Mary Tyler Moore: *Change of Habit* (1969)
Frank Sinatra: *The Miracle of the Bells* (1948)
Deborah Kerr: *Black Narcissus* (1946)
William Holden: *Satan Never Sleeps* (1962)
Karl Malden: *On the Waterfront* (1954)

Kris Kristofferson – the Kid can sing

Rod Steiger – there are some films you just have to wash your hands of

Ten actors who've played Henry VIII

Robert Shaw: *A Man For All Seasons* (1966)
Charlton Heston: *The Prince and the Pauper* (1977)
Lyn Harding: *Les Perles de la Couronne* (1937)
James Robertson Justice: *The Sword and the Rose* (1953)
Paul Rogers: *The Prince and the Pauper* (1962)
Charles Laughton: *The Private Life of Henry VIII* (1933)
Montagu Love: *The Prince and the Pauper* (1937)
Sid James: *Carry On Henry* (1971)
Keith Michell: *Henry VIII and His Six Wives* (1972)
Richard Burton: *Anne of the Thousand Days* (1969)

The last temptation of an actor – ten who've played Jesus Christ

Robert Powell: *Jesus of Nazareth* (1977)
Jeffrey Hunter: *King of Kings* (1961)
Brian Blessed: *Son of Man* – TV (1969)
Frank Finlay: *Son of Man* – Theatre (1969)
Max Von Sydow: *The Greatest Story Ever Told* (1965)
Chris Sarandon: *The Day Christ Died* (1980)
Ted Neeley: *Jesus Christ Superstar* (1973)
David Essex: *Godspell* (1971)
Willem Dafoe: *The Last Temptation of Christ* (1988)
Enrique Irazoqui: *The Gospel According to St Matthew* (1964)

Ten actors who've played Pontius Pilate

Rod Steiger: *Jesus of Nazareth* (1977)
Basil Rathbone: *The Last Days of Pompeii* (1935)
Arthur Kennedy: *Barabbas* (1962)
Telly Savalas: *The Greatest Story Ever Told* (1965)
David Bowie: *The Last Temptation of Christ* (1988)
Jean Gabin: *Golgotha* (1935)
Donald Pleasance: *The Passover Plot* (1976)
Hurd Hatfield: *King of Kings* (1961)
Keith Michell: *The Day Christ Died* (1980)
Richard Boone: *The Robe* (1953)

Ten actors who've played kings

Alec Guinness: Charles I (*Cromwell*, 1970)
Vincent Price: Charles II (*Hudson's Bay*, 1940)
Kenneth Branagh: Henry V (*Henry V*, 1989)
Nigel Terry: King John (*The Lion in Winter*, 1968)
Peter O'Toole: Henry II (*Becket*, 1964)
Laurence Olivier: Richard III (*Richard III*, 1955)
Sean Connery: Richard I (*Robin Hood: Prince of Thieves*, 1991)
Robert Morley: George III (*Beau Brummell*, 1954)
David Hemmings: King Alfred (*Alfred the Great*, 1969)
James Robertson Justice: Edward VII (*Mayerling*, 1968)

Marlene Dietrich, Queen Goddess

Ten screen ghosts
Kay Hammond: *Blithe Spirit* (1945)
Daryl Hannah: *High Spirits* (1988)
James Stewart: *It's a Wonderful Life* (1946)
Alec Guinness: *Star Wars* (1977)
Warren Beatty: *Heaven Can Wait* (1978)
Jóhn Gielgud: *Arthur 2* (1989)
Ernest Borgnine: *The Ghost of Flight 401* (1978)
Rex Harrison: *The Ghost and Mrs Muir* (1947)
Robert Donat: *The Ghost Goes West* (1936)
Robert Montgomery: *Here Comes Mr Jordan*
    (1941)

Ten actors who've done Shakespeare on screen
Mel Gibson: *Hamlet* (1990)
Victor Spinetti: *The Taming of the Shrew* (1967)
James Cagney: *A Midsummer Night's Dream*
    (1935)
Richard Briers: *Henry V* (1985)
Marlon Brando: *Julius Caesar* (1953)
Martin Shaw: *Macbeth* (1971)
Laurence Harvey: *Romeo and Juliet* (1954)
Orson Welles: *Othello* (1952)
Toyah Wilcox: *The Tempest* (1980)
Charlton Heston: *Antony and Cleopatra* (1972)

Warren Beatty adding an extra dimension to Dick Tracy

Ten actresses who've played queens
Vanessa Redgrave: Queen Mary (*Mary Queen of
    Scots*, 1971)
Greta Garbo: Queen Christina (*Queen Christina*,
    1933)
Katharine Hepburn: Eleanor of Aquitaine (*A
    Lion in Winter*, 1968)
Marlene Dietrich: Catherine the Great (*The
    Scarlet Empress*, 1934)
Genevieve Bujold: Anne Boleyn (*Anne of the
    Thousand Days*, 1969)
Jeanette Charles: Elizabeth II (*Marcia*, 1977)
Deborah Kerr: Catherine Parr (*Young Bess*, 1953)
Helena Bonham Carter: Lady Jane Grey (*Lady
    Jane*, 1986)
Jane Asher: Jane Seymour (*Henry VIII and His
    Six Wives*, 1972)
Elsa Lanchester: Anne of Cleaves (*The Private
    Life of Henry VIII*, 1933)

Elementary, my dear Mason – Christopher Plummer and James in *Murder by Decree*

Larger than life – ten actors who've played cartoon characters

Michael Keaton: Batman
Robin Williams: Popeye
Christopher Reeve: Superman
Anouska Hempel: Tiffany Jones
Lynda Carter: Wonder Woman
Lou Ferrigno: The Incredible Hulk
Warren Beatty: Dick Tracy
Helen Slater: Supergirl
Glynis Barber: Jane
Monica Vitti: Modesty Blaise

The Basil Rathbone factor – ten other actors who've played Sherlock Holmes

Roger Moore: *Sherlock Holmes in New York* – TV (1976)
Peter Cook: *The Hound of the Baskervilles* (1977)
Stewart Granger: *The Hound of the Baskervilles* – TV (1972)
Nicol Williamson: *The Seven-Per-Cent Solution* (1976)
Christopher Plummer: *Murder By Decree* (1978)
Ian Richardson: *The Sign of Four* (1983)
Christopher Lee: *Sherlock Holmes and The Deadly Necklace* (1962)
Peter Cushing: *The Hound of the Baskervilles* (1959)
Michael Caine: *Sherlock and Me* – TV (1988)
John Neville: *A Study in Terror* (1965)

Ten actors who've played Dr Watson

Colin Blakely: *The Private Life of Sherlock Holmes* (1970)
Thorley Walters: *The Adventures of Sherlock Holmes' Smarter Brother* (1975)
Nigel Bruce: *The Adventures of Sherlock Holmes* (1939)
James Mason: *Murder By Decree* (1979)
Campbell Singer: *The Man With the Twisted Lip* (1951)
Donald Houston: *A Study in Terror* (1965)
Dudley Moore: *The Hound of the Baskervilles* (1978)
André Morell: *The Hound of the Baskervilles* (1959)
Reginald Owen: *Sherlock Holmes* (1932)
Robert Duvall: *The Seven-Per-Cent Solution* (1976)

Ten films you must have in your video collection

Telephone Girl, Typist Girl, or Why I Became a Christian (India, 1925)

In My Time Boys Didn't Use Haircream (Argentina, 1937)

I-Ro-Ha-Ni-Ho-He-Yo (Japan, 1960)

Rat Fink A Boo Boo (USA, 1964)

The Nasty Rabbit (USA, 1965)

Ha Ha, Hee Hee, Hoo Hoo (India, 1955)

Why the UFOs Steal Our Lettuce (West Germany, 1979)

The Film that Rises to the Surface of Clarified Butter (USA, 1968)

Egg! Egg? (Sweden, 1975)

The Birth of New Zealand (New Zealand, 1922)

Ten rock stars who became actors

Mick Jagger: *Ned Kelly* (1970); *Performance* (1970)

David Bowie: *The Man Who Fell to Earth* (1976); *Merry Christmas Mr Lawrence* (1982); *Into the Night* (1985); *Absolute Beginners* (1986); *The Last Temptation of Christ* (1988); etc.

Adam Faith: *Stardust* (1974)

Sting: *Quadrophenia* (1979); *Brimstone and Treacle* (1982); *Dune* (1984); *Plenty* (1985); *Stormy Monday* (1988); etc.

Roger Daltry: *McVicar* (1980); *Buddy's Song* (1991)

Ringo Starr: *Candy* (1968); *Caveman* (1981)

Bob Dylan: *Pat Garrett and Billy the Kid* (1973)

Sonny Bono: *Escape to Athena* (1979); *Hairspray* (1988)

Art Garfunkel: *Bad Timing* (1980)

John Lennon: *How I Won the War* (1967)

Mick Jagger, sheep fighting man

Greta Scacchi on the road to Nairobi

Name-changing – how ten film titles changed in transit

Jaws: *The Teeth of the Sea* (France, 1975)
Blazing Saddles: *Springtime for the Sheriff* (Sweden, 1974)
A View to a Kill: *The Indestructible Iron Man Fights Against the Electronic Gang* (Hong Kong, 1985)
White Mischief: *On the Road to Nairobi* (France, 1987)
Baby Boom: *Who Called the Stork?* (Latin America, 1987)
Outrageous Fortune: *Nothing but Problems with This Guy* (Germany, 1986)
Friday the 13th: *Tuesday the 13th* (Latin America, 1980)
Planes, Trains and Automobiles: *Better to Be Alone than in Bad Company* (Spain, 1987)
Tough Guys: *Archie and Harry, They Can't Do It* (Germany, 1986)
Couch Trip: *Talk to My Psyche, My Head is Sick* (France, 1988)

What are you doing here? Ten people you didn't know had appeared in 'Carry On' movies

Jill Ireland: *Carry On Nurse* (1959)
Patrick Mower: *Carry On England* (1976)
Joan Hickson: *Carry On Regardless* (1961)
Bob Monkhouse: *Carry On Sergeant* (1958)
Anton Rodgers: *Carry On Cruising* (1963)
Milo O'Shea: *Carry On Cabby* (1963)
Warren Mitchell: *Carry On Cleo* (1964)
Elke Sommer: *Carry On Behind* (1976)
Phil Silvers: *Carry On Follow That Camel* (1967)
David Essex: *Carry On Henry* (1971)

Mad Max Malvinas

The day war broke out – ten movies that were showing when the Second World War started

Q Planes starring Laurence Olivier
Idiot's Delight starring Clark Gable
On Borrowed Time starring Lionel Barrymore
Ask a Policeman starring Will Hay
The Spy in Black starring Conrad Veidt
Goodbye Mr Chips starring Robert Donat
That Certain Age starring Deanna Durbin
Golden Gloves starring Victor McLaglen
Beau Geste starring Gary Cooper
I Was a Spy starring Herbert Marshall

Ten movies that were showing when the Falklands War started

Reds starring Warren Beatty and Diane Keaton
Evil Under the Sun starring Peter Ustinov
Raiders of the Lost Ark starring Harrison Ford
Whose Life is it Anyway? starring Richard
    Dreyfuss
Sharky's Machine starring Burt Reynolds
Kurosawa's *I Live in Fear*
Death Wish II starring Charles Bronson
Chariots of Fire starring Nigel Havers and Ben
    Cross
Absence of Malice starring Paul Newman
Mad Max II starring Mel Gibson

Pretentious, moi? Children's names chosen by actors

China (David Soul)
Elijah Blue (Cher)
Sage Moonblood (Sylvester Stallone)
Rumer (Bruce Willis and Demi Moore)
Dakota Mayi (Don Johnson and Melanie Griffith)
Rain (Richard Pryor)
Langley Fox (Mariel Hemingway)
Free (Barbara Hershey)
Statten (Nicholas Roeg and Theresa Russell)
Harley Moon (Martin Kemp)

Ten movies that were showing when the Gulf War started

Walt Disney's *Fantasia*
Ghost starring Patrick Swayze and Demi Moore
Hunt for Red October starring Sean Connery
Air America starring Mel Gibson
Ken Loach's *Hidden Agenda*
The Sheltering Sky starring Debra Winger
Stephen Spielberg's *Memphis Belle*
Reversal of Fortune starring Jeremy Irons
The Hot Spot starring Don Johnson
Narrow Margin starring Gene Hackman

'That's enough Tarzans for now' – ed.

The loincloth that covers a multitude of movies – ten Tarzan movies to end all Tarzan movies, with any luck

The Adventures of Chinese Tarzan (1940)
Tarzan and the Mermaids (1948)
Tarzan Goes to India (1962)
Rocket Tarzan (1963)
Tarzan and Delilah (1964)
Tarzan and King Kong (1965)
Tarzans Kampf Mit Dem Gorilla (1968)
Tarzan in Fairyland (1968)
Tarzan the Swinger (1970)
Tarzan and the Valley of Lust (1976)

The curse of Bram Stoker – ten movies to set Dracula's creator spinning in his crypt

Billy the Kid Versus Dracula (1965)
Batman Fights Dracula (1967)
Dracula Meets the Outer Space Chicks (1968)
Dracula the Dirty Old Man (1969)
Deafula (1974)
Dracula's Dog (1978)
Love at First Bite (1979)
Dracula Bites the Big Apple (1979)
Dracula Sucks (1980)
Dracula Blows his Cool (1982)

W.C. Fields, a nose by many other names

Now starring in a song near you – ten actors immortalised in pop
'Bette Davis Eyes' (Kim Carnes)
'Robert De Niro's Waiting' (Bananarama)
'He Looks Like Spencer Tracy Now' (Deacon Blue)
'Michael Caine' (Madness)
'Hey Bogart' (Nik Kershaw)
'Errol Flynn' (Dogs D'Amour)
'The Ballad of Me and Shirley Maclaine' (Danny Wilson)
'Marlon Brando' (Elton John)
'John Wayne is Big Leggy' (Haysi Fantayzee)
'James Dean' (The Eagles)

Ten characters from W.C. Fields' movies
Elmer Prettywillie
Egbert Sousé
T. Frothingell Bellows
Larson E. Whipsnade
Harold Bissonette
Charles Bogle
Otis Criblecoblis
Mahatma Kane Jeeves
Cuthbert J. Twillie
Professor Eustace McGargle

Ten capital movies

Moscow on the Hudson (1984)
An American in Paris (1951)
Mr Smith Goes to Washington (1939)
Tony Rome (1967)
Our Man in Havana (1960)
Funeral in Berlin (1966)
Storm Over Lisbon (1944)
The Purple Rose of Cairo (1985)
An American Werewolf in London (1981)
Bagdad Café (1988)

Spot the product – ten movies in which Pepsi-Cola has been 'placed'

Crocodile Dundee 2 (1988)
Hairspray (1988)
Bright Lights, Big City (1988)
Wall Street (1987)
Stand and Deliver (1988)
Throw Momma From the Train (1987)
Back to the Future (1985)
Cobra (1986)
Batteries Not Included (1987)
The Golden Child (1986)

Typecasting call for actresses

Plucky, put-upon country girl: Sissy Spacek
Plucky, feisty country girl: Sally Field
Cute girl-next-door: Meg Ryan
Woman succeeding in a man's world: Sigourney
  Weaver
Woman struggling in a man's world: Anjelica
  Huston
Jewish Princess: Bette Midler
Young and kookie: Emily Lloyd
Middle-aged and kookie: Goldie Hawn
Older and kookie: Shirley Maclaine
Anyone foreign/anyone else: Meryl Streep

Meryl Streep – crazy name

Goldie Hawn – crazy girl

Michael J. Fox, wisecracking all the way to the bank

Typecasting call for actors

Young wisecracking hero: Michael J. Fox
Middle-aged wisecracking hero: Harrison Ford
Manic nice guy: Robin Williams
Quiet, alienated loner: William Hurt
Seedy Englishman: Denholm Elliott
Upper-class Englishman: Edward Fox
Working-class man under 5 foot 6: Bob Hoskins
Laid-back hero who undermines the system: Jack Nicholson
All-purpose psychopath: Donald Pleasance
Any film requiring an actor who is not Dustin Hoffman or Tom Cruise: Michael Caine

'This one's for Johnny . . .' Ten movies that made him famous

Johnny Angel (1945)
Johnny Cool (1963)
Johnny Concho (1956)
Johnny Trouble (1956)
Johnny Eager (1942)
Johnny Guitar (1953)
Johnny Dangerously (1984)
Johnny Dark (1954)
Johnny Nobody (1960)
Johnny Handsome (1989)

Ten immortal 'Carry On' characters

Gripper Burke (Bernard Bresslaw) *Carry On Loving* (1970)
Gladstone Screwer (Sid James) *Carry On Again, Doctor* (1968)
Constable Constable (Kenneth Connor) *Carry On, Constable* (1960)
Khasi of Kalabar (Kenneth Williams) *Carry On Up the Khyber* (1968)
Francis Bigger (Frankie Howard) *Carry On, Doctor* (1968)
Citizen Camembert (Kenneth Williams) *Carry On Don't Lose Your Head* (1966)
Hengist Pod (Kenneth Connor) *Carry On, Cleo* (1964)
Sid Boggle (Sid James) *Carry On Camping* (1969)
Marshal P. Knutt (Jim Dale) *Carry On, Cowboy* (1966)
W.C. Boggs (Kenneth Williams) *Carry On At Your Convenience (1971)*

Ten headlines inspired by Steven Spielberg

Unclothed Encounters of the Bird Kind (*Mayfair*)
Close Encounters of the Furred Kind (*Evening Standard*)
Close in Contours (*The Guardian*)
Close Encounters with the Third Reich (*Vogue*)
Benign Encounters of the Rono Kind (*Daily Mail*)
Clothes Encounter (*The Guardian*)
Close Encounters of a Caring Kind (*The Listener*)
Illegal Aliens of the Third Kind (*Omni*)
Philosophical Encounters of the First-Class Kind (*Radio Times*)
Benign Intentions of a Dazzling Kind (*The Times*)

Ten movies from one to ten

One Flew Over the Cuckoo's Nest (1975)
Two Mules for Sister Sara (1969)
Three Men and a Baby (1987)
Four for Texas (1963)
Five Easy Pieces (1970)
Six Bridges to Cross (1955)
Seven Samurai (1954)
Eight and a Half (1963)
Nine to Five (1980)
'10' (1979)

Ten Bond girls' names

Honeychile Rider: Ursula Andress in *Dr No* (1962)
Domino: Kim Basinger in *Never Say Never Again* (1983)
Tiffany Case: Jill St John in *Diamonds are Forever* (1971)
Tatiana Romanova: Daniella Bianchi in *From Russia with Love* (1963)
Holly Goodhead: Lois Chiles in *Moonraker* (1979)
Pussy Galore: Honor Blackman in *Goldfinger* (1964)
Mary Goodnight: Britt Ekland in *The Man with the Golden Gun* (1974)
Kissy Suzuki: Mie Hama in *You Only Live Twice* (1967)
Solitaire: Jane Seymour in *Live and Let Die* (1973)
Octopussy: Maud Adams in *Octopussy* (1983)

Kim Basinger – all the 7s and a double 6

Tom Selleck, Magnum Farce

Ten stars whose first big break was in TV

Michael J. Fox (*Family Ties*)
Danny De Vito (*Taxi*)
Bruce Willis (*Moonlighting*)
John Travolta (*Welcome Back Kotter*)
Goldie Hawn (*Rowan and Martin's Laugh-In*)
Ted Danson (*Cheers*)
Mary Tyler Moore (*The Dick Van Dyke Show*)
Alan Alda (*M.A.S.H.*)
Tom Selleck (*Magnum*)
John Goodman (*Roseanne*)

Ten quintessential Christmas movies

It's a Wonderful Life (1946)
Miracle on 34th Street (1947)
White Christmas (1954)
Scrooge (1951)
Santa Claus (1985)
The Wizard of Oz (1939)
The Holly and the Ivy (1952)
Christmas Eve (1947)
Tenth Avenue Angel (1948)
Christmas in Connecticut (1945)

Ten unforgettable Royal Film Performances

A Matter of Life and Death (1946)
To Catch a Thief (1955)
West Side Story (1962)
Romeo and Juliet (1968)
The Prime of Miss Jean Brodie (1969)
Close Encounters of the Third Kind (1978)
Kramer versus Kramer (1980)
Chariots of Fire (1981)
A Passage to India (1985)
Empire of the Sun (1988)

Ten forgettable Royal Film Performances

Because You're Mine (1952)
Rob Roy the Highland Rogue (1953)
Beau Brummel (1954)
Sammy Going South (1963)
Love Story (1971)
Lost Horizon (1973)
The Slipper and the Rose (1976)
Silver Streak (1977)
Evil Under the Sun (1982)
Table for Five (1983)

Eddie Murphy – from one night a week to *48 Hours* with Nick Nolte

The forgotten ones – ten people who got joint billing but aren't so well remembered

Christopher Jones with Sarah Miles, Robert Mitchum (*Ryan's Daughter*, 1970)

Vivian Blaine with Marlon Brando, Frank Sinatra, Jean Simmons (*Guys and Dolls*, 1955)

Richard Beymer with Natalie Wood (*West Side Story*, 1961)

Jennie Linden with Glenda Jackson, Oliver Reed, Alan Bates (*Women in Love*, 1969)

Jules Munshin with Frank Sinatra, Gene Kelly (*On the Town*, 1949)

Brad Dexter with Yul Brynner, Steve McQueen, Robert Vaughn, Charles Bronson, James Coburn, Horst Buchholz (*The Magnificent Seven*, 1960)

Dee Hepburn with John Gordon Sinclair (*Gregory's Girl*, 1980)

Christopher Gable with Twiggy (*The Boyfriend*, 1971)

Paul Le Mat with Ron Howard, Richard Dreyfuss (*American Graffiti*, 1973)

Louise Fletcher with Jack Nicholson (*One Flew Over the Cuckoo's Nest*, 1975)

Karen Lynn Gorney with John Travolta (*Saturday Night Fever*, 1978)

Ten stars who got their break on *Saturday Night Live*

Dan Aykroyd
Jane Curtain
Bill Murray
Chevy Chase
Gilda Radner
Jim Belushi
Joe Piscopo
Billy Crystal
John Belushi
Eddie Murphy

Ten actresses known by their nicknames

Clara Bow: the It Girl
Veronica Lake: the Peekaboo Girl
Brigitte Bardot: the Sex Kitten
Jean Harlow: the Platinum Blonde
Ann Sheridan: the Oomph Girl
Mary Pickford: America's Sweetheart
Joan Crawford: the Clothes Horse
Lana Turner: the Sweater Girl
Betty Grable: the Pin-up Girl
Marie McDonald: the Body

Ten questions which innumerable viewings of *The Great Escape* do not resolve

Why is Steve McQueen allowed to wear 1960s casual clothing?

Why is James Coburn cast as an Australian?

If everyone knows that Richard Attenborough is 'Big X', why bother to give him a codename?

If Steve McQueen can escape so easily under the wire, why bother to go to the trouble of digging a tunnel?

Why don't the Germans get suspicious of British officers raking over dirt?

Why does Gordon Jackson always fall for the old trick of answering in English when wished a pleasant journey by the Gestapo officer?

Anyone for decaff? Steve McQueen, Gordon Jackson and Richard Attenborough in *The Great Escape*

Aren't there kinder ways for James Garner to point out Donald Pleasance's myopia than to trip him up?

And if he's so short-sighted, why did Pleasance go up in the reconnaissance plane for a joyride in the first place?

Why don't we actually see Hardy Amies making David McCallum's suit?

Why does Charles Bronson try to join a group of Russian POWs at the start of the film?

AND FINALLY...
FIFTY WAYS TO SELL
A MOVIE

'Condemned by Cardinal Spellman' (*Baby Doll*, 1956)

★

'The picture with something to offend everyone' (*The Loved One*, 1965)

★

'If this doesn't make your skin crawl . . . it's on too tight!' (*Black Christmas*, 1975)

★

'Two million years in the making!' (*The Animal World*, 1956)

'You have everything to lose but your mind!' (*Asylum*, 1972)

★

'Some days business is good – and some days it's murder!' (*The Big Sleep*, 1977)

★

'At last, the book that couldn't be written is the motion picture that couldn't be made!' (*Myra Breckinridge*, 1970)

The motion picture that *was* made – John Huston and Raquel Welch in *Myra Breckinridge*

'If this one doesn't scare you . . . you're already dead!' (*Phantasm*, 1979)

★

'She was the woman of his dreams. She had large dark eyes, a beautiful smile and great pair of fins' (*Splash!*, 1984)

★

'Everything that makes life worth leaving!' (*Vault of Horror*, 1973)

★

'Guaranteed not to make you think' (*Fighting American*, 1924)

★

'Growing! growing! growing! When will it stop?' (*The Amazing Colossal Man*, 1957)

★

'He is a shy schoolmaster. She is a music hall star. They marry and immediately have 283 children – all boys!' (*Goodbye Mr Chips*, 1969)

★

'See it with someone who can carry you home!' (*Macabre*, 1958)

★

'See Don Ameche invent the telephone' (*The Story of Alexander Graham Bell*, 1939)

★

'The third dimension is terror!' (*Jaws 3-D*, 1983)

'Nothing says goodbye like a bullet!' (*The Long Goodbye*, 1973)

★

'The next scream you hear may be your own!' (*Play Misty For Me*, 1971)

★

'10,965 pyramids! 5,337 dancing girls! One million swaying bulrushes! 802 sacred bulls!' (*The Egyptian*, 1954)

★

'The management reserves the right to put up the lights any time the audience becomes too emotionally disturbed. We urge you not to panic or bolt from your seats' (*The Black Scorpion*, 1957)

★

'As big as the ocean!' (*The Caine Mutiny*, 1954)

★

'Dramatic magnificence, spectacular splendour, riotous joy, tigerish rage, undying love, terrifying tempests, appalling earthquakes!' (*King of Kings*, 1927)

★

'Love-starved women in uniform . . . Men whose days are numbered . . . thrown together in the mad whirl of life and death, love and laughter that is war.' (*Women in War*, 1940)

Jaws, the fin end of the wedge

Making a killing – Warren Beatty and Fay Dunaway in *Bonnie and Clyde*

'If you miss the first five minutes you miss one suicide, two executions, one seduction, and the key to the plot!' (*The Kremlin Letter*, 1970)

★

'A town – a stranger – and the things he does to its people! Especially its women!' (*Picnic*, 1956)

★

'In making this film, MGM feels privileged to add something of permanent value to the cultural treasure house of mankind!' (*Quo Vadis*, 1951)

★

'He felt the lash of Nazi terror! When they torture you for hours and then sneer that your mother is held hostage . . . you think you'll go mad!' (*I Escaped From the Gestapo*, 1943)

★

'When poets love . . . heaven and earth fall back to watch.' (*The Barretts of Wimpole Street*, 1934)

★

'They do things you've never seen before!' (*Boom!*, 1968)

★

'A slithering slimy horror spawned from the poisons of pollution' (*Godzilla vs the Smog Monster*, 1972)

'They're young . . . they're in love . . . and they kill people!' (*Bonnie and Clyde*, 1967)

★

'Just when you thought it was safe to go back in the water' (*Jaws 2*, 1978)

★

'There are three sides to this love story' (*Kramer versus Kramer*, 1979)

★

'No woman ever loved such a man! The whole world waited while he made love!' (*Death Takes a Holiday*, 1934)

★

'Out of the dark fantastic madness of his science he created her – the panther woman – throbbing to the hot flush of new-found love!' (*Island of Lost Souls*, 1933)

★

'There's nothing but trouble in Paradise when the bandleader tries to make love to a whole sister act – simultaneously!' (*And the Angels Sing*, 1944)

★

'The only thing more terrifying than the last twelve minutes of this film is the first eighty!' (*Suspira*, 1976)

'In space, no one can hear you scream!' (*Alien*, 1979)

★

'We are not alone . . .' (*Close Encounters of the Third Kind*, 1977)

★

'You don't assign him to murder cases – you just turn him loose!' (*Dirty Harry*, 1971)

★

'To have seen it is to wear a badge of courage!' (*Frankenstein*, 1931)

★

'A love story every woman would die a thousand deaths to live!' (*Jane Eyre*, 1943)

★

'Only the rainbow can duplicate its brilliance!' (*The Adventures of Robin Hood*, 1938)

★

'The two most gorgeous humans you've ever beheld – caressed by soft tropic winds – tossed by the tides of love!' (*Bahama Passage*, 1941)

'It's tremonstrous! The absolute apex of the super-shivery!' (*The Black Cat*, 1934)

★

'First they moved (1895)! Then they talked (1927)! Now they smell!' (*Scent of Mystery*, 1959)

★

'Meet the girls with the thermo-nuclear navels! The most titillating time bombs you've ever been tempted to trigger!' (*Dr Goldfoot and the Girl Bombs*, 1966)

★

'Where there's smoke, there must be someone smoking!' (*Easy Living*, 1937)

★

'Sister, sister, oh so fair, why is there blood all over your hair?' (*Whatever Happened to Baby Jane*, 1962)

★

'Garbo talks!' (*Anna Christie*, 1930)

Garbo – no small talk from a big star

Final credits

The authors used many books in compiling *Movielists*, but, obviously, they used some more than others. Therefore here – in no particular order – are the top ten books they used (all of which are thoroughly recommended).

Halliwell's Film Guide: Leslie Halliwell (Paladin)
I'm Not One to Gossip But . . . : David Hartnell with Brian Williams (Futura)
Elliot's Guide to Films on Video: John Elliot (Boxtree)
Who Played Who on the Screen: Roy Pickard (B T Batsford)

The Guinness Book of Movie Facts & Feats: Patrick Robertson (Guinness)
60 Years of the Oscar: Robert Osborne (Equation)
20th Century Quotations: Frank S Pepper (Sphere)
The Penguin Dictionary of Modern Humorous Quotations: Fred Metcalf (Penguin)
The Guinness Encyclopedia of Hollywood: Scott Siegel and Barbara Siegel (Guinness)
Halliwell's Filmgoer's Companion: Leslie Halliwell (Grafton Books)